What Others Are Sayi

"I took Michelle's coaching program. Everyone should take it. My sales also increased 76 percent. Michelle is the next Tony Robbins."

—*J. Lewakowski*

"I'd been going through challenging experiences in my professional life that were impacting me negatively in all areas of life—even inducing clinical depression . . . I was given the tools to 'win' and am succeeding now . . . until forever."

—*K. Sellers*

"Michelle and IPV have done a great job working with our staff to develop much-needed skills in time planning, managing personal stress, empathy, listening, and many other skills. Her direct approach and dedication to helping people succeed have been a welcome resource for our team."

—*J. Thomas*

"Her skills are above par: Michelle's instruction is engaging, and her knowledge is wide-ranging, providing a wealth of information for building self-growth. Her compassion is contagious."

—*B. Hines*

"I found the tools Michelle provided essential to my personal growth, focus, and realization of the importance of time management. A worthwhile investment in myself."

—*C. Krawczyk*

"I feel so much more positive, optimistic, happy, and driven to accomplish my goals! The encouragement, thoughtful accountability, and incredible information she shared put me on the path to success, and I now feel UNSTOPPABLE!"

—*A. Criswell*

"I've seen a positive, dramatic change in how I view myself and the world . . . I highly recommend Michelle . . . to anyone wanting to know how to achieve success and take control of their life."

—R. Rice

"She was specifically mentioned as the best part of the training program. She raises the productivity of those she is around."

—T. Lynema

"Michelle will leave you awed by your team's improvement . . . their efficiency and productivity, their new and improved attitudes, their changed lives. Michelle is a leader of leaders."

—L. Lyons

"Michelle has a proven track record of success in her professional career and excels at building integrated, high performing teams. She can work with any group of people and optimize their performance, which is a gift that seems to come naturally to her."

—W. DeJong

REFRAME

AND

REWIRE

REFRAME

AND

REWIRE

Greatness Through Daily Routine

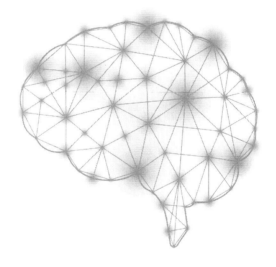

MICHELLE L. STEFFES

credo
house publishers

Reframe and Rewire
Copyright © 2018, 2021 by Michelle L. Steffes
All rights reserved. First edition 2018 (formerly *Your Journey to Greatness through Routine*).
Second edition 2021.

Published in the United States of America by Credo House Publishers,
a division of Credo Communications LLC, Grand Rapids, Michigan
credohousepublishers.com

ISBN 978-1-62586-184-9

Cover and interior design by Frank Gutbrod
Editing by Shelly Beach and Linnae Conkel

Printed in the United States of America
Second Edition

CONTENTS

START HERE

Chances are you are reading this book because you know what you want out of life but feel unsure how to get there.

You're not alone. I stood right where you are once, along with roughly 85 percent of the population, according to statistics.

Since then, I've spent over two decades building and leading teams, pouring into multitudes of clients, and investing over 10,000 hours of personal study on the brain science behind habits and routines. Over the course of two decades, I discovered that there really *is* a pattern to developing greatness from within.

During my journey, I rebounded from a serious career setback and doubled the profits of my new business in only six months. This was the result of creating a solid new daily routine and sticking to it. Furthermore, I've seen dramatic changes in myself, as well as my clients, in both personal and professional mindsets. These changes restored relationships, massively increased income, produced multiple promotions, and created wholeness in mind and body, along with many other benefits.

My style of helping people win is unique because I paint a clear picture of what happens inside your mind and body as I walk you through a metamorphosis of complete change. At every step, I also give you the "why" behind the "what," so you fully comprehend the brain science and psychological processes that are at work changing you. You also discover solid applications that transform old habits into brand new ways of thinking, acting, and being.

With your desire to succeed, determination to win, and passion for a better version of YOU, your time has come to learn how to build a new daily routine that will equip you to alter your future forever! Get ready!

Get ready to become "unstuck" in your life or career!
Get ready to take your life from "okay" to "amazing"!
Get ready to overcome past regrets, hurts, and bad habits!

Learn the science behind creating habits, along with helpful insights, practical tools, and needed steps for a new daily routine. Whether you're seeking new opportunities or restoring lost ones, you'll find the information in this book to be truly transformational.

Discover ways to retrain your brain, alter your physiology, and expand your potential.

Be inspired by case studies that demonstrate how others accomplished new daily routines as you see the program in action.

Be inspired by the power of creating a Vision Statement (Chapter Two), the art and influence of Cognitive Restructuring (Chapter Three), the necessity and impact of Cognitive Consonance (Chapter Five), the freedom of how to get Unstuck (Chapter Seven), and the insight that comes when you master Energy, Focus, and Time (Chapters Eight and Nine), along with many other tools and applications to equip you on your journey.

When you understand both brain science and body chemistry, creating a new routine that positively influences who you want to become not only makes sense, but also becomes palpable and attainable.

Throughout this book, unique, scientifically backed information and practical steps will give you a brand-new outlook on what your life/career could be. You will also find inventories, assessments, thought-honing assignments, downloadable tools, new routines, greatness tips, quotes, charts, and other resources to further empower you.

Whether you are seeking to advance to a more successful career or are struggling with vision for your future, this step-by-step guide will help you raise your standards of performance, take you to a level you've never imagined before, and energize you to keep moving forward. So turn the page and get started now!

PART ONE

THE PSYCHOLOGY AND SCIENCE OF GREATNESS

CHAPTER ONE

FIRST STEPS

*"If you always do what you've always done, you
will always get what you've always got."* [1]

—HENRY FORD

Real, lasting change cannot occur until you first assess your daily routine. This begins by taking a hard look at your career and life choices from a different perspective. The daily habits, rituals, mindsets, and behaviors we unconsciously choose often keep us from achieving our greatest potential.

Your first step is discovering why you are where you are. Become a student of yourself by studying how you think, what you talk about, and how you spend your personal and professional time. As you continue reading, you'll discover the valuable science behind my training, and you will receive clear guidelines on how to fulfill training goals.

In the first section of each chapter, you will find client case studies. Although clients' names are changed, the stories are true. Each study demonstrates how the impact of a routine for success can transform areas of life faster than anything else we do.

CASE STUDY #1
JEN'S STORY

Around Christmas time, Jen was feeling desperate for solutions. She'd been passed over at least 3 times in her job of twenty-seven years, and her marriage was not what she'd dreamed it would be. Each day, she mindlessly "went through the motions" of her daily routine.

Her husband was also depressed and often spoke about his unhappiness at work. He couldn't seem to please his boss. As she listened to her husband, Jen feared he might be on the brink of losing his job. She felt lost and began wondering if there was a future for her in her life and career.

Jen began spending time reminiscing about how pleasurable life used to be. In earlier years, she'd been jovial, fun, and loved life! Now, life seemed to keep dealing her the same hand with the same monotonous results. She found herself struggling to get up in the morning to face another predictable, drab, purposeless day. She'd hit the snooze button multiple times, then rush to prepare for another pressure-filled day. She became overcome with anxiety about her daily routine before she even left home, and stress remained on her drive to work.

In an effort to create a sense of purpose, Jen often signed up for volunteering and other activities. But each attempt to fill the void in her life only resulted in negative inner dialogues that inhibited her ability to find joy or fulfillment, even when she showed kindness to others.

While at a volunteer event, Jen shared her frustrations with her friend Tracy. In response, Tracy told Jen about recent changes she'd made in her daily routine, what she was doing to create a new perspective on life, and how these things were positively affecting her career. Tracy's changes had influenced her sales to rise more in four months' time than in her first three sales years combined.

Jen was inspired!

Upon hearing the secret of Tracy's transformation, Jen felt a spark of hope and resolved to take the same actions.

In the beginning of her new journey, Jen discovered she needed to make many changes in her daily routine and her thought life. At first, these things seemed a bit overwhelming, but she stuck with the process. In a short time, Jen recognized that the changes, although seemingly small, made a significant difference in her perceptions on life, relationships, career, success, and even challenges. As she continued implementing her new routine, joy returned to her life, and the heavy weight of hopelessness and despair slowly lifted.

After barely four weeks of diligence to her new routine, Jen began receiving questions from her supervisor and other people about the difference they saw in her. Their comments made her even more excited and hopeful about her future. Life became a joyous adventure again, and her transformation continued.

Jen was enthusiastic about this revelatory new program and resolved to continue developing her new daily routine and make it permanent. Within three months, she was awarded the task of launching a new program at her workplace.

Even more amazingly, Jen reconnected with her boss. Several months earlier, their relationship had become disjointed and communication had become difficult, if not impossible. With her new routine in place, Jen compassionately and respectfully reached out to her boss and began working on restoring their relationship. With newfound confidence and boldness, she was able to present a well-written proposal and to begin working on a project that would eventually transform the entire organization. As time passed, Jen felt a greater and greater sense of value and purpose.

Jen's new lifestyle seemed to be affecting everyone in her path, as if her transformation was contagious. At home, things were evolving. Several weeks into her transformation, Jen's husband was still struggling with hardships at his job, which sent him further into despair. While Jen's life was taking a turn for the better, his life and career were in a downward spiral.

However, after Jen's fourth week working her plan, things began to shift quickly for both herself and her husband. Because of the changes in Jen and her husband's second-hand exposure to her new routine, he began to journey out of depression. Within two months, he was searching for a new occupation and eventually found a new and better job. Jen and her husband are now both happily employed and excited about their future.

Today, Jen continues her new daily routine and remains resolved to keep striving for daily growth. She now understands how to daily empower herself with a completely different mindset.

Jen received two promotions and initiated a new program for her company. She is now an established Professional Development Director. She mediates for top leadership within her company, and executive leadership has recognized her for her accomplishments. Jen has created a new life and new perspectives. She is steadily increasing her potential in all aspects of life and career.

And the best part? Jen is no longer "invisible" in her work environment or anywhere else. She states, "I'm no longer invisible, but a force to be reckoned with!"

Please note: You will discover the changes Jen made throughout the pages of this book. As you read, pause for every tip, question, and assignment in order to learn how you can achieve great things by altering your routine.

TAKE ONE STEP AT A TIME

Dedicate your first week to building your foundation. Progress is never made in an instant but through many intentional decisions and changes over a course of time.

- **Determine**
- **Believe**
- **Apply**

Determine to set your heart in a direction that will daily prime you with new and fresh ideas.

Believe in your ability to achieve greatness.

Apply new perceptions that you commit to learn every day.

Don't get overwhelmed . . . take ONE STEP at a time. As you saw in Jen's story, the greatest achievements result from the smallest beginnings. Each small change you make will lead to big shifts in your life, both professionally and personally.

The great news is that you can customize your new routine in a manner that won't interfere with your current obligations or commitments. Work on goals and inspire change by exchanging the mundane for the purposeful.

We spend valuable time on many things that could be considered purposeless. Things such as Facebook, Twitter, Pinterest, emails, texts, television, and many other activities can become useless distractions. If we're honest about our schedules, we'll discover opportunities to become more intentional about the way we live, how we think, and who we want to become.

FIRST ASSIGNMENT

Clear your mind of obstacles and inhibitions. This includes negative thinking, self-criticism, anger, fear, judgment, worry, and task lists. Then write out the goals you want to accomplish in each of the following areas:

- **Personal Development**
- **Professional Development**
- **Material Goals or Gain**

Think carefully and prioritize the items in each list, beginning with the goal that will take you the furthest toward personal fulfillment the fastest.

Remember, you spend 8 hours sleeping and 8 hours working. This leaves you with 8 hours to work on personal growth and development goals.

> **REFRAME AND REWIRE TIP #1**
> Think about effective ways to reprioritize your current routine. We never successfully develop new habits when we try to "fit them in" with our old routine. We never have enough time. We must *create* time for anything new.

Here are three examples of how to find time to develop new habits:

1. If you drive a meager 12,000 miles per year and exchange what you currently listen to in the car with educational material, in 3 years you will have listened to an equivalent of 2 years of college classroom instruction.

2. If you spend only 20 minutes per day reading on topics of interest, your reading will equate to twenty, 200-page books per year. Working on yourself instead of watching TV or spending time on social media is only one of many ways you can create drastic change.

3. If you want to adopt an exercise routine, you can awaken 20–30 minutes earlier. In time, you'd become accustomed to rising earlier and would begin enjoying the benefits. In fact, you would alter your physiology (body chemistry), creating an addiction to your new morning routine.

SUCCESS IS A JOURNEY

John Maxwell and Brian Tracy are two highly successful authors, speakers, and teachers who have created winning routines. Each sets goals, stays persistent, and keeps moving forward. Both Maxwell and Tracy view success as a personal journey, not a destination.

According to Dictionary.com, the definition of *journey* is "traveling from one place to another, usually taking a rather long time; trip, passage, or progress from one stage to another." Every day of our lives we are either moving forward or backward, based on our actions. But *we are never sitting still.*

When we think we're sitting still, we're actually regressing and will NEVER make any headway. When we sit still, we actually move backwards as a result of stagnancy.

Imagine your journey to reframe and rewire as a train trip. Unless you pour coal or wood into the engine, the train will never have the energy to move to its next destination. The actions we take each day for growth provide fuel for our journey. How far or how fast we travel is completely up to us.

Taking responsibility for our success and progress always begins with us. Regardless of where we are now and what's happened to us in the past, we can choose to pour on the coal and start moving forward. On the other hand, we can choose to blame others, make excuses, or find reasons why we aren't moving. Even in cases where we have been betrayed, rejected, abused, abandoned, or otherwise mistreated, the responsibility to move forward is still ours. Until we decide to shovel our own coal, we will never see progress.

It's important to remember that everyone has a story. Everyone has been hurt, treated unfairly, or damaged at some point in their lives. But ultimately, our journey is not about what goes on outside of us as much as what goes on *inside us* in response to life circumstances.

Each day you choose to take positive action, you **raise your life standards**. Determine to change your daily habits and unleash opportunities instead of struggling with the price of unintentional living. As you do this, you will increasingly experience more of the following:

- Deeper Inner Peace and Confidence
- Certainty about Your Abilities and Your Future
- Creativity and Vigor on the Job
- Clarity and Direction
- Excitement and Zeal about Overcoming New Challenges
- Resolve and Determination to See Your Vision Fulfilled
- Improved Health: Mentally, Emotionally, Spiritually, and Physically

Human physiology teaches that when we allow fear or stress to overcome us, two hormones are released: adrenaline and cortisol. Adrenaline is a superpower of sorts, and it's typically one reason people indulge in extreme sports or watch horror movies. The "high" they experience from the adrenaline rush can be addictive. In cases of true emergencies or life-threatening circumstances, adrenaline provides power surges that can be nearly super-human in nature.

However, the level of stress or fear we allow to overtake us on a day-to-day basis determines the amount of cortisol that is released in our bodies. When this happens, cortisol paralyzes portions of the frontal lobe in our brains, which is referred to as "the executive center." The response is called "fight or flight."

In situations where we are authentically in danger, the release of these chemicals can be lifesaving. Think of the mother whose child is trapped under a car in an accident. She will do anything to save her child. She runs over, picks up the car almost effortlessly, and pulls her child to safety. She is able to do so because of supernatural strength provided by adrenaline. At the same time, cortisol paralyzes the reasoning portion of her frontal cortex, so the mother doesn't consider the reality that she cannot pick up a car.

This chemical response is also true regarding soldiers on the battlefield or when we are threatened and need to make decisions without time to reason. However, if cortisol remains in our brains too long or at levels that are too high, it can cause self-destructive side effects and debilitating symptoms of chronic stress.

SYMPTOMS OF CHRONIC STRESS

- Inadequate sleep
- Poor eating habits
- Emotional distress
- Reduced attention
- Decreased perception (brain fog)
- Loss of short-term memory
- Reduced learning receptivity and retention
- Difficulty communicating clearly

THESE SYMPTOMS ARE A RESULT OF

- Decreased regulation of cortisol
- Increases in glucocorticoids
- Cellular changes in the hippocampus[2]

TOP 10 STRESS-RELATED ILLNESSES

1. Heart Disease
2. Asthma
3. Obesity
4. Diabetes
5. Headaches
6. Depression
7. Reflux and Irritable Bowel Syndrome
8. Alzheimer's
9. Accelerated Aging
10. Premature Death[3]

WHO OR WHAT IS IN CONTROL?

Two major red flags reveal when we are not in control: anxiety and frustration. These responses indicate that we're *either not* choosing to empower ourselves with a daily routine that creates a positive mindset, *or* we are succumbing to the dictates of our circumstances. In other words, we are living reactively instead of intentionally.

Psychologists generally agree that an estimated 80–85 percent of the population lives "reactively." When we're reactive, our responses are controlled by what I often refer to as a "two-year-old" mindset. We react to situations emotionally, neglecting the power we possess to control how we respond. We're manipulated by our feelings in the moment and do not take time to be emotionally intelligent about what is really happening or the outcome we want.

Unless we take control, this reactive pattern will often resurface when we face challenges, making us "runaways" from opportunities for growth and advancement.

It's time to take back control!

ROUTINE BUILDERS FROM CHAPTER ONE

1. Evaluate your current daily routine. List habits that are time "wasters" or activities that may be inhibiting your growth:

   _____

   _____

   _____

   _____

2. Exchange the mundane for the purposeful in your everyday life or career. List new habits you'd like to adopt to replace those listed in #1:

   _____

   _____

   _____

   _____

3. From the habits you listed in #2, list tasks you must schedule into your daily routine, and prioritize them in order of importance:

   _____

   _____

   _____

   _____

GREATNESS TIP 1

To consistently reframe and rewire, you must be open to altering your current schedule.

GREATNESS TIP 2

Managing your schedule to become more productive and fulfilling is the first step in reducing daily stress. As you design your lists, choose only tasks and activities that will give you a sense of daily purpose and progress.

CHAPTER TWO

THE BRAIN SCIENCE
BEHIND HABITS

"Guard your heart with all diligence
for out of it flow the issues of life!"

—PROVERBS 4:23

Understanding basic brain functions and the neuroscience behind forming habits empowers us to take action with fewer reservations. When we become aware of cognitive responses, we realize how plausible it is to rewire our brain and create new neural pathways and mindsets. The only caveat is our determination to persist, no matter how we may feel or what circumstances arise to dissuade us. Most of us have heard that we can alter our mindset within 21–30 days. Interestingly, this philosophy stems from our knowledge of "neuroplasticity," which will be explained throughout this chapter.

Almost 95 percent of our daily decisions, actions, feelings, and beliefs originate in our subconscious mind, according to numerous cognitive studies performed over many decades. Our subconscious mind is actually 30,000 times more powerful than our conscious mind![4]

Over the course of your lifetime, thousands of ideas, thoughts, beliefs, and skills have entered your mind and created new neural pathways and networks. These neural networks compose your subconscious. You have been growing neural pathways and networks since your conception.

Our neurons grow "dendrites" each time we're exposed to something new. A dendrite is a pinkish-brown, protein substance that grows and lengthens until it connects with the axon of another neuron. This process occurs because electrical impulses in the brain target specific sections of neurons, often based on previous beliefs or concepts. From infancy to adulthood, each time we learn something new, we create new connections. Each connection is called a synaptic connection. An adult brain over the age of 35 can have as many as one thousand-trillion synaptic connections.[5]

Networks of neural pathways are related. They determine how we think, how we process, and how we perceive the world around us. The more thoughts we have about a particular subject, idea, issue, or skill, the more neural connections will form, creating multiple networks in our brain that are bent in a particular direction. Over a lifetime, we have built every network in our brain, whether positive or negative. Think of the many influences you have been exposed to, including ideals, education, tragedies, people, and experiences. In many cases, if something tragic happened in our past, we grew a large neural network in that area because we thought about it for weeks, months, years, or even decades.

Painful, vivid experiences are another determining factor for large neural networks. When strong emotions occur, floods of hormones are released in our brains, leaving a powerful "imprint" with deep roots that become difficult to extract. Each negative or positive neural network we create dramatically affects our perceptions on life, success, wealth, work, people, self, religion, the world, etc. The good news is that we can alter or transform these networks in the same manner they were created.

Who do you want to be? What do you want to do, have, or accomplish? The changes you desire will begin with the new information you program into your daily subconscious thoughts. The easiest and most effective way to produce a new thought life is through a change in daily habits.

Remember, you did not create negative neural networks overnight, so you will not alter them overnight. Although it takes 21–30 days to initiate necessary changes in perception, it can take up to 3 cycles or 63–90 days to develop change into a sustained habit. In cases where the networks deeply connect with many other networks, it can take much longer to alter them. Real, lasting change requires long-term commitment, combined with constant, consistent reinforcement over an extended period of time.

If you are willing to follow through with the suggestions made in this book and commit to daily brain retraining, dramatic changes can be made at an accelerated pace. In fact, newer networks that were more recently formed are often easier to change. Networks that began earlier in life can take much longer to transform.

Case after case proves that ALL networks (e.g., habits) can be changed if you are willing to be consistent, regardless of how long the process takes.

CASE STUDY #2
TOM'S STORY

After devoting twenty-six years to working in public service, Tom was facing a crossroads in his life and career. His children were almost grown, and he had a desire to do something greater.

In the fall, he was required to attend mandatory staff training. He assumed it would be about something he'd heard before. He didn't realize that what he was about to hear would change his life forever.

I'd been commissioned to provide a two-day training for the city's civil servant team. The topic was "Resilience in Times of Change." The core of this training revolved around brain science and altering old mindsets. During this training, Tom learned that through daily subtle yet powerful changes in his routine and habits, he could alter his destiny. He was enticed to the point of seeking information about how he could get help to create the change he was so hungry for. This was the beginning of a brand-new journey of discovery and growth for him.

The first thing Tom was required to do was develop a personal vision statement, along with five specific goals that would help him achieve his vision. Tom immediately set a goal of earning a prestigious position within a year's time. It seemed like a steep goal, but he really wanted this promotion for himself, his family, and his community. Furthermore, he was committed to the process and willing to put in the work to make it happen.

The next step was to begin putting together a customized new daily routine that would take Tom there. Day after day, he worked diligently, adopting new habits that would serve to "retrain his brain." He also worked hard on relationships in his personal and professional life. He desired to engage with people more deeply and show more compassion. The more Tom succeeded at making an impact in his relationships, the more driven he became to take his new routine to the next level, and the easier it seemed to achieve his goals. After a couple of weeks, others began noticing dramatic and positive changes in Tom, too.

One of the important things Tom had to learn was the principle of sowing and reaping, sometimes referred to as "karma" or the "law of attraction." This principle is universal and applies to all of us, whether we acknowledge it or not. Stated simply, we either attract opportunities for ourselves or push them away, based on the impact we make in the world around us, whether good or bad.

Three weeks into Tom's efforts towards massive change, a new position he was hoping for unexpectedly opened up, and it was within travel distance of his home. Tom was beside himself as he considered the possibilities. Things were happening much faster than he'd predicted, and with some coaxing, he took a chance and pursued the opportunity.

Although the application process was tedious and time consuming, Tom was patient. Sticking to his new daily routine had helped him feel confident and bold. After weeks of waiting, the prospective employer announced that Tom was among the top three of over 40 nationwide candidates who had applied for the position. This seemed too good to be true . . . Even his family agreed that his selection felt surreal. But the ordeal was not over yet. Tom still had to overcome two more hurdles, and his competitors seemed much more qualified.

The pressure was intense. Tom struggled with juggling the obligations of his current position while he continued the application process. However, his diligence to his new daily routine gave him the confidence he needed not to choke under the pressure.

The next day, the news he'd been waiting for came in. Tom had won the position and was beside himself with gratitude! He paused to look back and realized that he'd reached his goal in only five weeks! He was amazed at what he'd accomplished and the new man he'd become to his family, friends, and community. He'd been awarded the position that he'd made his goal to win in one year in less than two months!

Tom discovered that the key to his success was more about WHO he'd become than the position he'd won.

Tom adopted a routine that anyone is capable of keeping, and the results for others can be just as amazing!

THE KEY TO TRANSFORMATION— SYNAPTIC PRUNING

The next principle we will discuss in the brain science of creating habits is key in understanding cause and effect in transformation. This powerful key is linked to a term called "synaptic pruning," which is an important part of neural plasticity, a term we mentioned earlier.

Synaptic pruning is a process in which the brain literally sheds or eliminates older, weakened neural synaptic connections. These connections are usually unused and older because they have been superseded by new information that has negated old beliefs or ideals. During this process, old, useless pathways literally fall off neurons to make room for new connections.

Here's an example to help you understand how this process works:

Let's say you travel to Europe to stay for thirty days. If you are from the Western world, you will have to learn how to drive on the left side of the road, instead of the right.

At first, it will seem incredibly awkward and somewhat terrifying. However, after approximately three weeks of driving, the process will become more natural to you.

Why? Because your brain stopped electrical impulses from "feeding" the neural pathways that programmed you to drive on the right side of the road. At the same time, your brain developed new neural pathways to program you to drive on the left side.

Upon returning home, you find yourself feeling awkward all over again because you must reverse the thinking process. The only difference you may find is that since your deepest connections or networks were developed while you were driving on the right, reversing the synaptic connections will take less time and seem easier than when you arrived in Europe and learned to drive on the left for the very first time.

An interesting take-away from this example is that *you will likely feel quite awkward when you first begin a new habit or new routine designed to initiate change.* This is why the majority of the population gives up on new year's resolutions within two weeks. But if we want to accomplish real change, *we need to commit to daily change over a minimum of three weeks before we notice any convincing results.*

Like Tom, when we are intentional about changing our habits and daily routines and determine to stay with our commitment no matter what it takes, we will watch our greatest dreams unfold before our eyes. We must be willing to change what we listen to, think about, and pay attention to. When we become aware of what influences us, we can drastically transform our minds and create new perceptions.

This same phenomenon occurs when we learn a new skill, study for a new occupation, or challenge ourselves with new knowledge. The brain also responds in the same manner when our eyes are opened to a philosophy or a truth that we formerly rejected, due to wrong suppositions or poor influences from our past.

SECOND ASSIGNMENT

Using the goals you wrote down in Chapter One, write out a vision statement for yourself. Condense it down into one or two sentences. Make sure it begins with "I am." Then pay attention to everything you allow into your thought life. Write down ideas about how you can feed your subconscious new thoughts that will align with your vision.

Choose philosophies, educational options, and concepts that will push you forward and keep you on track. Write your vision on small cards so you can refer to it, read it, and speak it often. Study it as if you were taking an exam you must absolutely pass. These practices will require discipline at first, but real change will become obvious within 21–30 days, after which your routine will become easier. Results will depend upon how diligent you are in making decisive and significant positive changes in your routine. Your statement will help you determine if your choices in activities are moving you forward or holding you back from seeing your vision come to fruition.

reframeandrewire.com

> **REFRAME AND REWIRE TIP #2**
> When writing your vision, think about four strengths you possess that will get you to your ultimate destination in life or your career. Under each strength, write out four of each: goals you want to work on and resources that will aid you in the process.
>
> Taking inventory will give you a clearer picture of how much you already have going for you. It will also reveal capabilities and resources you forgot about or laid aside.

THE SCHOOL OF SUCCESS

As with any area where you want to grow, your success will require a sacrifice of your time and energy.

- If we determine to lose weight, we will have to change our eating habits and lifestyle.
- If we want to earn a college degree, we will have to work diligently, regularly attend classes, study hard, and complete assignments and exams.
- If we want a job promotion, we have to work hard, learn and fulfill our position effectively, and go the extra mile.
- Try to look at your journey as a "school of success." If you want to take your life and your career to the next level, you will need to:

- Be deliberate and methodical in managing your time.
- Set measurable goals and take steps to complete them.
- Develop a vision and use it to keep your focus.
- Be open to changing or adding new habits and routines.
- Maintain a resolve to Do Whatever It Takes!

The process begins when we "feed our brain" exactly what it needs to grow and avoid things that cause it to feel fearful, doubtful, or uncertain. One philosophy I find useful when I need to do whatever it takes is to keep telling myself, "If you are too comfortable, you are not growing."

The earlier example about driving in Europe shows us that, if we are truly honest with ourselves, we can look back and see that the uncomfortable moments in life are where we will find the most growth.

Years ago, I was at a crossroads in my career that forced me to make some very difficult decisions about my current daily routine. Just like Tom, I wanted to take my career to the next level, and financially, I had to. I was working morning until night, trying to pull all the pieces together to make it happen. I'd made progress, but it wasn't happening fast enough. Furthermore, the progress I'd made seemed meager for the effort I was putting forth. Doubt and fear badgered me as I pushed on, using my experience, education, and raw willpower to bring about some kind of success.

A day of decision finally came for me. I clenched my fists, gritted my teeth, and said to myself, "No more! I will not lose one more thing! I am going to do whatever it takes, no matter what it costs me!"

That decision influenced me to start looking at my routine, habits, and vision from a different perspective. I was no longer "just interested" in going to the next level: I was committed. This mind shift was the foundation for drastic change.

At that point, I began a "Morning Power Hour" that altered my state of mind and infused me with a sort of "superpower" that became the foundation to multiplying my business by 200 percent in less than six months!

MY MORNING POWER HOUR

Building a brand-new routine takes discipline, commitment, and perseverance.

When I first developed the morning portion of my new daily routine, I determined to wake up an hour and a half earlier each day (4:30 a.m.) and create my own "power hour." I filled the time with exercise, prayer, affirmations, and insightful podcasts. The mental exercise prepared me to start my day with an outstanding mind set, while the physical exercise empowered my brain and body to become more alert, creative, and clear. Within a few weeks, I noticed more energy to tackle the day, as well as relief from brain fatigue and fog.

Both physical and biological evidence prove that physical exercise triggers the pituitary gland, which then floods our bodies and our brains with endorphins. This produces an "energized mental high."

In fact, studies show that a good dose of endorphins can be 200 times more powerful than morphine.[6] (This is covered in greater detail in later chapters).

In the beginning, following through with my Power Hour was not easy for me. For the first month, I stood sleepy-eyed in the bathroom, arguing with myself and wanting to go back to bed. Sometimes I even succumbed to the temptation, convincing myself that sleep was more important.

After approximately four weeks of persistence, I began to notice a difference, and my "why" (vision) became bigger and bigger. The combination of my "why" and my newly forming habit increased my determination to stick with it, in spite of how I felt on any particular morning.

This is how I was able to increase my business by 200 percent in such a small about of time. Years later, I still maintain this incredibly valuable routine Monday through Friday, and I love it!

Never give up. The payoff is worth it!

What do you do when you arise in the morning? What time do you start your day? Do you find the beginning of your day energizing and positive, or hurried and negative? Perhaps it's time for a change.

ROUTINE BUILDERS FROM CHAPTER TWO

1. Your thoughts build negative and positive neural networks over a lifetime. Consider taking a 48-hour Thought Diary Challenge. Use the lines below or a journal to record the types of thoughts that run through your mind most of the time:

    _____

    _____

    _____

    _____

2. In Chapter One, you were asked to create new habits for managing your time more effectively and intentionally. The same can be said of your thoughts. Take a few moments to list things in your life or career that you can and should be happy about. Now challenge yourself to cultivate the positive instead of the negative:

    _____

    _____

    _____

    _____

GREATNESS TIP 3

Writing your personal Vision Statement will empower you with focus and clarity.

GREATNESS TIP 4

Directing your mind to focus on things that make you feel grateful or accomplished is the next step in reducing daily stress. As you design days focused on constructive thinking, resolve to choose only activities and entertainment that will push you forward into your destiny.

CHAPTER THREE

RETRAINING YOUR BRAIN THROUGH COGNITIVE RESTRUCTURING

Retraining your brain after a lifetime of wrong perceptions not only requires reframing and rewiring but also "tools" to daily empower you to keep your focus. Many useful tools can be implemented to help you move from level to level while staying the course.

Altering your neural pathways, and ultimately your mindsets, requires cognitive restructuring. Cognitive restructuring can accelerate the change process as you learn how to alter your perceptions. Altering perceptions is a powerful foundation of Cognitive Behavioral Therapy, a practice often used by counselors to reverse negative tendencies in their patients. Below is a helpful four-step guide to cognitive restructuring. For a printable worksheet, visit:

reframeandrewire.com

THIRD ASSIGNMENT
FOUR-STEP GUIDE TO COGNITIVE RESTRUCTURING
Step #1: Describe in writing a recent occurrence that produced negative thoughts, fear, apprehension, or anxiety for you.

Step #2: Record the negative thoughts you experienced at the time of the situation or event.

Step #3: Remove yourself from all emotional ties to and presuppositions about the event, and then write out a few objective observations.

Step #4: Consider a list of positive responses you can choose to apply, based on the rational observation in step #3.

Situation/ Event	Negative Thoughts	Rational Observation	Positive Response

Another powerful tool I recommend for reframing and rewiring is daily affirmations. I'm not referring to simply repeating a few positive statements every day. When you merely think or speak positive words that don't agree with your core beliefs, your affirmations will accomplish nothing. This kind of mental posture is known as "cognitive dissonance." This term was first mentioned in earlier chapters, but now we will dive deeper into what it means.

Affirmations can only be an effective form of cognitive restructuring when "cognitive consonance" is present, which Businessdictionary.com defines as "a state of harmony and internal consistency arising from compatibility among a person's attitudes, behavior, beliefs, and/or knowledge." This definition is the opposite of cognitive dissonance.

Therefore, simply speaking affirmations is not enough to create change. You must speak affirmations AS IF you truly believe, using your mind, heart, and emotions. When you first begin using affirmations, you will likely feel a mixture of cognitive consonance and cognitive dissonance, which makes the process seem difficult and useless at times. However, when you engage all three simultaneously with visualization, you powerfully influence your neural pathways at their deepest level.

Affirmations that are reinforced frequently and consistently will eventually influence your heart and mind to come into agreement with your core values and align with what you are saying.

At this point, you may be asking, "So how does cognitive restructuring make things happen in the exterior world around me?" To answer that question, I refer to another great proverb which states, "As a man thinks in his heart, so is he". Proverbs 23:7

Think for a moment about someone you know who is wealthy or successful. Now think about the types of people and opportunities they attract. What if they awoke one day and started thinking they were poor and struggling in life, relationships, and their career?

If they persisted down this path and began making decisions that aligned with this new belief system, over time, their thoughts would change who was attracted to them and would eventually ruin their financial state.

In the same way, we can be certain that how we dress, act, speak, think, and live affects who we attract, what opportunities come our way, and whether or not we see our goals come to fruition.

Are you still struggling with this philosophy? An article published in the *British Journal of Sociology* states that "sudden wealth is often associated with social and psychological risks." Interviews with lottery winners show that they use "earmarking" prize money as a strategy for avoiding the pitfalls associated with lottery wins and sudden wealth. Classifying their large sum of money into normative categories—paying off debt, saving for designated goals, cash for the future, giving, and personal spending—allows them to budget their funds in *a familiar and successful way*, in contrast to winners to see themselves as "rich" and spend in an entirely new way.[7]

Many people who have budgeted all their lives can successfully manage sudden wealth because they already have the skills. However, those who never learned to manage money will experience cognitive dissonance with wealth management, causing them to make devastating and uninformed decisions with their fortunes. In effect, they took a short cut to riches without simultaneously changing their subconscious attitudes and skills needed to manage their wealth.

Remember, our neural connections are the strongest in our subconscious. Therefore, because people who do not have cognitive wiring from their past to manage a windfall of wealth, they end up losing it all, and more.

CASE STUDY #3
KIM'S STORY

Kim had a strong desire to make a difference in the lives of others. In both her life and work, she demonstrated excellence. In fact, others often referred to her as an "overachiever."

Kim worked for an organization that was involved with the public on many levels. Her position required her to spendlong hours creating opportunities to interact and build relationships with the community. She was also accountable to the leadership team, so her name was well-known within the organization.

After seven years of dedicated work, the winds of favor shifted for Kim. This confused her because, in her mind, she'd done all she could to maintain strong and influential rapport and had been conscientious about how she presented herself to leadership and the community.

However, growing resentment seemed to be forming against Kim from some of the leaders in the organization. In spite of her efforts to be cooperative and kind, matters only became worse. It soon became evident that Kim was allowing the tension in the atmosphere to affect her, causing her mental anguish and distress. Every effort she made to keep peace and do her job seemed futile.

Kim decided she needed help from outside her work environment to regain her confidence, which had been broken by months of unmerited pressure and animosity. She attended an event for women where she heard a message I shared on "Avoiding Burnout."

Because Kim felt she was on the fringes of burnout, the presentation resonated with her. What stood out most to her was information she heard about retraining the brain and altering the subconscious to become more resilient. She reached out to me immediately after the event. Kim wanted to find out if it was truly possible to train her brain, and, if so, what she needed to do. After I spoke to her for a short time, she made an easy decision.

In short order, Kim began her journey of altering her perceptions, changing her routines, and improving her inner dialogues. Within the first week of her brain training, she noticed a gradual but significant return of confidence. After two weeks, others began to inquire about where she had gotten her infusion of inner strength and sense of well-being. Colleagues in her department knew of the injustices done to Kim and were happy for her as she continued to rediscover her strength. Other people who had been spiteful to her before, dug their heels in and continued their attempts to bring her down.

Despite the animosity she was facing, Kim continued to reframe and rewire, strengthening her resolve to be the best version of herself she could be. She fulfilled every task and assignment given to her with excellence and integrity. Kim also worked hard to empower others and demonstrated kindness to everyone on her team at work.

In the end, Kim was let go. But instead of feeling devastated, she felt strangely relieved and content. She knew she'd maintained her state of mind and integrity through the transitions with her employer and left with dignity.

Kim began using her gifts and influence, along with her newfound strength and resilience, to build the business of her dreams. Today, Kim is empowering others to win, and her new business is steadily growing. She recently launched an online video broadcast that spotlights the other people's success and reports positive local news.

Kim often reflects about how far she has come: "I thank God for the important changes in my routine during some of the most difficult weeks of my life—changes that propelled me forward and altered my destiny."

Kim learned that empowering others always begins with empowering ourselves to win, and no one can take that from her.

A DEEPER LOOK AT THE SUBCONSCIOUS MIND

Our subconscious is the total infrastructure of neural networks we've created since birth. Each new network affects our perceptions and behaviors. Some of the deepest and most influential networks in our mind develop out of tragedy and traumatic events.

Think about where you were when something horribly tragic happened in your life. The magnitude of that event, mixed with the feelings you experienced and the consequences that followed, became etched in your subconscious forever. The event can be vividly played back in the theatre of your mind whenever your senses, thoughts, or emotions are triggered. The strong feelings you had at that time created your powerful memories. Compound those feelings and memories with the thoughts that you most likely focused on for days, weeks, months, or even years after your tragedy, and you can see how even one trauma creates significant changes in your mindsets, sometimes even altering your core values.

In the same way, if we want to create positive thoughts, images, and beliefs about something, we must first alter our subconscious mind. We do this when we generate passion or positive emotion to accompany positive thoughts that, in turn, build positive neural pathways as new perceptions become seared into our subconscious mind.

For years, athletes have trained using this concept. They're asked to visualize themselves competing in the sport of their choice while they're hooked up to monitors and are asked to visualize positive emotions, thoughts, and feelings, as well as sights, sounds, smells, feelings, and the outcome they desire.

Devices track their vital signs, as well as their nerves and muscles. Amazingly, their vitals and muscle fibers react as if they were actually playing the sport itself. Study after study proves that athlete performance improves vastly and consistently using this type of visualization.[8]

Another example to consider is how the body reacts when we watch a horror movie or love story. Our heart rate speeds up; we may sweat, tense up, or even cry. This happens because our thoughts align with what's played on the screen. One scientific study concluded that the subconscious mind does not know the difference between an imagined event and an actual event.[9]

The *New England Journal of Medicine* cites a case of placebo knee surgery involving 165 patients with osteoarthritis. Patients were randomly divided into separate groups targeted to undergo different procedures and track the outcome of each group. Each group provided consent to participate in the study. We will call them Groups A and B.

Group A received standard knee surgery. Group B received placebo knee surgery in which 3 incisions, 1 centimeter long, were made in the knee and then stitched up, but no surgical procedure was done. Patients in both groups were monitored for 24 months, and data was collected in 3-month intervals. The results were conclusive, indicating that both groups experienced full recovery from the knee disorder.[10]

This study and multitudes of others reveal that what we perceive in our subconscious is the dominating factor in our outcome.

Applying this knowledge as you pursue new habits and develop your new daily routine can help you. You are designed to succeed. You have the power to determine your outcome. All you have to do is tap into the resources you were born with.

To assist you in the cognitive restructuring required to alter your subconscious, I am including a copy of the affirmations I use every day and offer to my clients. Download at:

reframeandrewire.com

Speak these affirmations WITH FEELING over yourself, twice daily for a minimum of 30 days. Personalize them with specifics that bring more meaning and targeted vision to each one.

THERE IS POWER IN "I AM"

I am blessed.	I am secure.	I am the right weight.
I am prosperous.	I am disciplined.	I am filled with gratitude.
I am calm.	I am focused.	I am compassionate.
I am healthy.	I am attractive.	The right people are in my future.
I am talented.	I am valuable.	The right opportunities are headed my way.
I am creative.	I am well-liked.	This is my year.
I am confident.	I am fun to be around.	Great things are going to happen to me!
I am an overcomer.	I have favor.	This is my day!

REFRAME AND REWIRE TIP #3

Just as your body needs healthy meals each day to maintain optimum performance, your mind requires quality nutrition. As you set up your new routine, view your new "mind diet" as a necessary discipline to achieving your desired result. Your mind, like your body, underperforms on a consistent diet of "junk food" such as TV, media, gossip, negative words, etc.

"Those who fail typically focus on the pain of change more than the end result."

ROUTINE BUILDERS FROM CHAPTER THREE

1. Cognitive restructuring is a powerful way to alter bad perceptions and retrain your brain. What mindsets block you from the right perceptions?

   _____

   _____

   _____

   _____

GREATNESS TIP 5

Ponder the mindsets you desire to change. Think about daily tools that will equip you to begin setting your vision in motion.

CHAPTER FOUR

THE GARDEN OF YOUR MIND

"Whatever a man sows, he will reap in return."

—GALATIANS 6:7

You express approximately 60,000 thoughts per day in the Garden of Your Mind. Are you tending weeds or seeds?

WEEDS

- Rehearsing the Problem
- Unforgiveness
- Self-Pity
- Entitlement
- Taking Offense
- Comparing Yourself to Others
- Feeling Inadequate
- No Vision—No Goals
- Feeling Stuck

SEEDS

- Brush the "Dust" Off and Move Forward
- Forgive Yourself and Others
- Take Responsibility for Your Own Success
- Ignore the Critics
- Get a Coach or Mentor to Hold You Accountable
- Motivate and Grow Every Day
- Create a Personal Vision and Set Specific Goals
- Empower Others Often

You were born with approximately one-hundred billion neurons in your brain and forty thousand in your heart. Each one is designed to process and store the information you select and feed into your brain. Gardens include healthy plants, as well as thorns and weeds (as listed in the beginning of this chapter). Even if you manage to change your perceptions and, ultimately, your subconscious, you still have to maintain the garden of your mind every day for the rest of your life.

CASE STUDY #4
JOHN'S STORY

John began his career excited about life and filled with anticipation of a great future! At a fairly young age, he began living the American dream. He married, had children, and quickly advanced up the ladder of success in his chosen career, grossing over 6 million in commissions in fewer than 10 years. At first, his world revolved around his marriage and his children. He celebrated rich moments with them and enjoyed their happy life together.

Over time, John's career consumed him. Things that were once important to him began to fade in significance, due to the busyness of life and work. Unknowingly, John began to tailor his daily routines to conform to his busy lifestyle. In his mind, everything in life was good. Each day he poured himself into his career without thought about his state of mind or the health of his family relationships. He ignored all the warning signs.

Whenever John was confronted with opposition to his lifestyle, he justified his choices by reasoning that his behavior was normal and responsible. Working hard to provide for his family made him feel secure. Despite continual requests from both his wife and children for genuine attention, John could never find the time. The efforts he did make were disconnected and brief, resulting in a growing chasm between himself and his family members, who desired the closeness they'd once shared with him.

The day came when, to John's shock and disbelief, his family walked out of his life. He'd unknowingly created multiple mindsets that blinded him to what was really happening. The break-up was no surprise to his wife and children, but this didn't ease the pain for anyone.

Over the next several years, John's life continued to spin out of control. He tried to deal with the pain of losing what was most precious to him and the confusion of how he'd gotten to this place.

With each passing year, John grew more discouraged and bitter, blaming events and people from his past for his misfortune.

In his brokenness and crushed state of mind, John adopted new habits as a way to cope and survive. Some of his habits drove him further away from who he once was, which led to more problems. Every area of his life spiraled downward.

In time, John realized how far he'd fallen from the confident, successful man he once was. He finally reached out for help. He read a story online about someone who found victory by making changes in their routine, their perceptions of life, and their career. He was inspired, and hope arose in his heart. He acted quickly and mustered the courage to take the needed steps to begin a new life.

At the beginning of his new journey, John was overwhelmed and discouraged by the details of his new life plan. The changes he needed to make in his daily routine seemed too difficult. He was afraid his journey would end in more disappointment. At the same time, John knew he needed to do something drastic and take a chance. He resolved it was worth finding out if the process would bring him the new life he was looking for.

At times John felt as if he wasn't accomplishing much. He felt frustrated with himself for his lack of discipline. However, he stuck with it, and things began turning around. In a few short weeks, John found himself slowly adapting to a new routine and lifestyle. Each day he put forth effort, he created new hope. As he persisted with his newfound daily routine, he grew stronger and more determined than ever to regain what he had lost.

John had developed deeply rooted, negative mindsets that made many days feel like an uphill battle. Yet, he persevered.

After five weeks of persisting, John began to see new signs of life in his finances, health, relationships, and himself. Looking back, he stated, "For the first time in years, I can see the light at the end of the tunnel."

After two years, John shared the following statement:

My past, my decisions, how I saw myself, and the issues I've had with acceptance and rejection, possibly enhanced by my adoption experience, have kept me from being all I really am to and for others. That began to change two years ago as I began to declare [my vision and affirmations] every day every time I saw them on my bathroom mirror, by my bed, by my workout apparatus, living room chair, refrigerator, kitchen cabinets, office desk, and wallet. [They] have all served as reminders of who I really am in Christ. It's now becoming evident to those on the outside who I have truly been inside all my life, I pray and believe.

After 10 years, John has overcome a number of obstacles in his world. He rebuilt his health and pushed himself to get back on track in life. He clearly understands the importance of maintaining priorities, sticking to his new daily routine, and maintaining a strong state of mind. He also realizes his journey is for life, and that the degree of his commitment will determine the degree of success he will retain.

John discovered that being aware of the weeds in his garden is never enough; we must daily take action to pull them out and replace them with good seeds. Only then can we rise above and win!

No matter how many weeds you pull, a garden will always need tending in order to produce a bountiful harvest. It will always be your responsibility to do whatever you can to guard against and extinguish thorns and weeds before they can grow. Once they're established, they choke out the healthy networks you and I work so hard to grow.

The "garden of your mind" must never be left unattended. No matter how healthy the garden may seem to be, weeds and thorns will always creep in and bring destruction, from poor health to depression and emotional upheaval to conflict affecting your career, relationships, well-being, and success.

> *"Whatever a man sows, he will reap in return."*
> —Galatians 6:7

Sowing good seeds to produce a healthy garden in your mind and your heart must be examined from multiple perspectives. The changes in your routine and habits will always affect your inner thought life, for better or for worse.

Now that you've written your vision, examine a few influences (or seeds). Analyze them to see if how you use them aligns with your vision or the "garden" you wish to produce. In other words, the influences in your daily life can be, but are not necessarily, all good things. You must regularly ask yourself what habits in your life may be "good seeds or bad seeds." It's also important to assess which seeds push you toward your destiny and which are time stealers or inhibit healthy growth in the garden of your heart and mind.

ENTERTAINMENT
Movies, media, video games, television

READING MATERIAL
Magazines, newspapers, books, articles, social media

PEOPLE

This includes friends, family, classmates, and co-workers (though you cannot always control some of these influences, you can limit the time you spend with them, or work on being an influencer instead of being influenced.)

MUSIC

Pay close attention to the messages they're sending.

SOCIAL MEDIA

Limit time spent unless it aligns with your vision, and monitor what you allow yourself to be exposed to.

EDUCATION OR INSIGHTS

YouTube, audiobooks, courses, training, or seminars. Are they pushing you toward your destiny?

When it comes to taking care of our garden and ensuring it matches our vision and pushes us toward our desired goals, we must do whatever is necessary to change our inner dialogue.

Therefore, a regular examination of our internal and external influences will not only reveal root causes of stress in our lives, it can help us prioritize what we become involved in and help us regain positive control of time. This assessment should be done periodically, especially if we are noticing "hiccups" in our progress.

FOURTH ASSIGNMENT

Take a brief inventory of seven inner and outer influences. Write them down, based on the following areas:

OUTER

- The people you spend most of your time with
- The types of games, media, or entertainment you indulge in
- Books or articles where you invest your time and thoughts

- Studies or lack of studies in areas you desire to grow in
- The amount of time you spend on social media
- The type of activities you are involved in
- The level of fitness you are committed to

INNER

- The ratio of positive vs. negative thoughts of the 60,000 you have per day
- The value of concepts you spend time thinking about
- The amount of time you spend creating lists and using your willpower to stay on track
- Visualizing consistently
- Time spent working on goals or dreams
- Regular time frames to unplug, spending "down" time to relax internally
- Time spent processing your mindsets with objectivity, maintaining a willingness to change them

Once you have written down your inner and outer influences, evaluate what changes you need to make and create a brief list of what you will work on. It should only take 20–30 minutes to complete this exercise. The difference it will make can save you hours of grief, fog, confusion, frustration, regret, and lost energy.

> ### REFRAME AND REWIRE TIP #4
> When we're aware of our thinking habits, we see cognitive change creating consistent progress in our thinking. Awareness of our progress inspires us to keep weeds out and sow productive seeds. This momentum pushes us forward faster than we expect.

This quote is a powerful principle in the analogy of the garden:

"Progress equals Happiness."
—Tony Robbins

ROUTINE BUILDERS FROM CHAPTER FOUR

1. If you did the assignment in this chapter, you should have created a list of habits and behaviors that must change. Look at that list and develop a plan of action for how you might maintain and nurture your garden every day going forward.

_____

_____

_____

_____

_____

_____

_____

_____

_____

_____

_____

_____

_____

_____

_____

_____

_____

_____

_____

_____

_____

_____

CHAPTER FIVE

HEART SCIENCE, ENERGY, AND THE LAW OF ATTRACTION

In the last chapter, we mentioned that your heart has 40,000 specialized neuron-like cells called cardiac intrinsic ganglia, or little brains of the heart.[11]

Each section of ganglia functions like neurons do but has a very special assignment that is distinctly different from the 100 billion neurons in your brain. Both your brain and your heart produce electromagnetic energy at a rate of approximately 400 billion actions per second. This energy is necessary for sustaining life, as well as housing creative ability. See Figure X (below) for locations of ganglia found in cadaver hearts.

Figure X[12]

According to the Director of Research at the HeartMath Institute, Rollin McCraty, a recognized global leader in emotional physiology, optimal function, resilience, and stress-management research, "The heart generates the largest electromagnetic field in the body. The electrical field as measured in an electrocardiogram (ECG) is about 60 times greater in amplitude than the brain waves recorded in an electroencephalogram (EEG)."[13] This energy or field is measured in magnetometers at a distance several feet away with a Superconducting Quantum Interference Device (SQUID).

In fact, the magnetometers are gauged by emotion. Such measurements were taken in an experiment at the HeartMath Institute, where tests were performed by provoking specific emotions in test subjects. The findings were eye-opening in regard to the importance of our state of mind and ability to master emotional intelligence.

During these tests, when subjects produced emotions such as love, joy, compassion, and gratitude, magnetometers indicated a range of approximately 500–600. When subjects produced emotions such as agreement, cooperation, and problem solving, magnetometers produced a range of roughly 200–350. In addition, when subjects produced emotions such as hate, envy, bitterness, and offense, magnetometers indicated a range of roughly 20–100.

So why is this information important in regard to building a new daily routine? The answer is quite simple. In fact, we don't necessarily need the statistics from the research mentioned above to figure it all out.

People can sense how we feel about them, another person, or a situation without us needing to say a word. Our heart produces unmistakable energy. Think about the last time you were with your significant other or perhaps a relative or friend who was angry with you. You may have walked into a room where the tension was high, or people were arguing. You could sense the bad energy in the room, even if they responded with a fake smile and said, "Everything is just fine."

You and I have the same ability as dogs do to sense fear. The big difference between us and dogs is that humans are not always "in tune" with this energy. Yet, we subconsciously use it every day to decipher and interpret others reactions or attitudes.

This energy is real. It can be the determining factor in whether you win over an employer in a job interview or make a sale in a business deal. Body language, facial expressions, and vocal tones are important, too. All of us know a "fake" when we meet one. They may have the right stance, posture, body language, and vocal tones, but if their hearts are not authentic, we pick up on it immediately.

Common sense tells us that when we master our emotional responses to all that life brings to us, we can choose an energy that will either attract or repel. In light of this information, ask yourself these questions:

1. If I choose to produce and maintain emotions such as love, joy, peace, patience, kindness, goodness, faithfulness, forgiveness, gentleness, and self-control and practice gratitude and compassion, will new doors of opportunity open for me in life and my career?

2. If I choose to produce and maintain emotions such as hatred, offense, insecurity, jealousy, bitterness, doubt, rage, anger, anxiety and a critical, judgmental mindset, will doors of opportunity close for me in my life and career?

CASE STUDY #5
TAMMY'S STORY

Being a single mom is challenging in today's world, but for Tammy, it was overwhelming. She couldn't figure out how to keep up with her full-time job, housework, shopping and errands, meet the needs of her family, and be the mom she wanted to be. After going through a tumultuous time with her ex-husband, she wasn't sure who she was supposed to be, much less try to meet others' needs.

For the sake of finding peace in her disrupted life, Tammy tried to please people and be the person everyone wanted her to be. This wasn't what she wanted, but she didn't know what to do with her future or how to make something better happen.

For Tammy, living had become more like survival. The idea of fulfillment seemed impossible. She only talked to a few close friends about her hardships, and one of them was her co-worker Robert. Robert always seemed positive and tried to encourage her. In fact, she was amazed at his relentless pursuit to reach his goals. Robert was on a journey to become the person he knew he wanted to be, and this inspired Tammy.

Eventually, Robert introduced Tammy to me, opening the door to her new journey.

First, Tammy developed a personal vision statement and selected goals that would push her toward her destiny. Each day, she incorporated a new way of living by implementing her new daily routine. She visualized a positive future filled with new ambitions, new hope, and an entirely new lifestyle.

The first thing Tammy wanted to change was her morning routine. Up until meeting me, she and her son had experienced extreme difficulties getting up early enough. Her son was frequently tardy to school, and Tammy's stress levels were also having an effect on his academic performance.

With her new daily routine in place, things began to change for Tammy and her son. She was rising early enough to enjoy her son and have time to prepare her mind and body for the day without feeling rushed.

Tammy became more focused and driven in pursuing her dreams. The more she poured herself into this pursuit, the more often positive things began to happen. People she'd never met before assisted her with portions of her vision. Opportunities began to appear, which built excitement and hope about her future.

At times, Tammy could barely contain herself with excitement. She lived in expectation of what might happen every day. The more excited she became, the easier it became to get up early, and the more frequently opportunities fell into her path.

Goal setting and pursuing a sound state of mind became sworn lifestyle changes for Tammy. As positive changes occurred, her son began setting goals and living with different perceptions, which caused his grades and demeanor to improve.

After five weeks, Tammy made an investment to continue with her program and a new daily routine. In the days that followed, she overcame confusion, hurt, and frustration from former relationships and even created a mutual agreement with her ex-husband. The agreement ended unrest and opened doors to a more cohesive interchange between them.

Tammy reversed almost every negative situation in her world and became excited about moving forward in life. She found out that when you change your perceptions and focus on your goals, good things come your way.

COGNITIVE DISSONANCE AND COGNITIVE CONSONANCE

We touched on Cognitive Dissonance and Consonance in Chapter Three when we discussed the power of affirmations. It's important that you grasp the science behind these terms and understand why you must make it your goal to create synchronicity between your heart and mind.

Since the heart and the brain both are designed with neurons or neuron-like cells and electromagnetic activity, they always communicate with each other. In fact, the connection between the two is vital to human emotion, as well as accomplishment in one's life and career.

Leon Festinger developed the Cognitive Dissonance Theory in 1957. This theory states that dissonance stems from unpleasant feelings of discomfort that result from holding two conflicting internal beliefs.[14]

I like to describe this feeling as *when your heart is not in agreement with your head.* The opposing term for this is Cognitive Consonance or, in my definition, *when your heart and your head are in complete agreement.*

To help you understand the role cognitive consonance plays in our ability to influence others and to be convinced ourselves, let's demonstrate this conflict parenthetically. A man desires to be a leader, so he signs up for multiple courses on leadership. He aces every course and is hired for an executive position, based on his impressive credentials. In fact, he appears to understand leadership even better than most of his peers and some of his superiors.

However, he lacks confidence, due to deeply rooted neural networks that cause him to frequently question his abilities. Despite his knowledge of leadership, he struggles daily with self-doubt, often tending to "people please" instead of lead. Furthermore, he portrays a sense of awkwardness and lack of authenticity in his communication with his team. As his team picks up on this, and they will, they instinctively lose trust in him and will eventually lose respect. He may experience moments or even days when his knowledge is enough to give him the confidence he needs to lead. However, the insecurities that lurk in his heart will frequently overpower the knowledge he has in his mind, stealing his ability to maintain a strong presence of leadership.

This scenario plays out in too many lives every day, at many different levels. Cognitive dissonance adversely affects relationships, success, sales, job performance, and a multitude of other life and career challenges.

Until cognitive consonance can be achieved, internal struggle will remain constant and relentless. In some cases, the dissonance can be absolutely maddening.

So how do we achieve cognitive consonance between our hearts and minds? This entire book, from beginning to end, is dedicated to helping you develop a daily routine that will empower you to build a new way of thinking and perceiving. Ultimately, reframing and rewiring can create cognitive consonance in areas of belief that held you back for years—areas where you lacked confidence or felt "stuck" or "cursed" or "not enough" because Mom, Dad, or Great Grandpa told you that is what or who you are.

It's also possible that something traumatic or hurtful happened to you, and you processed the experience in the worst way possible: by deceiving yourself about your true value and gifts. Through the natural inclination of human behavior, our subconscious often goes into a defensive survival mode. At these times, we can convince ourselves that something that is *entirely untrue* about our abilities, talents, intelligence, or value is true. If a new daily routine is not put into place and followed long-term, our false perceptions of self cannot be reversed or changed. Hence, our cognitive dissonance will continue.

At this point in the book, you should be contemplating the changes you must make if you want to achieve your full potential and rise to greatness. However, be warned that although the decision to move forward is the biggest step, it is only the *beginning* of the journey.

No matter who we are or what our current state of mind may be, we will always encounter "walls" or barriers that can inhibit our progress, such as:

- The atmosphere and culture we live in
- The fears that attempt to take over and stifle our faith and belief in who we are called to become
- Old patterns in our daily routine that pull us back to what is comfortable and block us from creating a new routine that can change our world
- The temptation to put other things ahead of our daily "training" because of a self-defeating mindset that our growth is not a priority
- A mindset of denial that tells us we cannot experience total transformation, even if we put forth daily effort
- Lack of practice using the mental faculties we're gifted with by our creator
- Strongholds that have been constructed in our minds by negative mindsets that need to be replaced and defeated

FIFTH ASSIGNMENT

In order to create powerful heart energy and develop cognitive consonance, we must raise new standards to live by and create an action plan to implement the changes we must make in our routine.

Below is a brief list of standards you can assess to develop a plan of attack! Consider what you must do to alter your heart energy and focus for each item on the list below. Then decide what new habits you will need to adopt in your daily routine to accomplish these changes.

- Health and Fitness
- Career Advancement
- State of Mind or Daily Motivation
- Goal Setting
- Relationships
- Sowing into the Lives of Others

REFRAME AND REWIRE TIP #5
Time Out for YOU! Managing "Heart Energy" and achieving cognitive consonance is not a "once and done" process but a lifelong commitment and lifestyle. Maintain the right heart energy by being intentional about every moment of every day.

ROUTINE BUILDERS FROM CHAPTER FIVE

1. Think about the opportunities, connections, promotions, or positions you desire to reach within 1–5 years. List them below:

_____

_____

_____

_____

_____

_____

_____

_____

2.   Based on the information in this chapter, what will you have to change in your life and your daily routine in order to see these doors open for you? List the changes you will have to make and how you will make them:

_____

_____

_____

_____

_____

_____

_____

_____

CHAPTER SIX

THE BIGGEST KILLER OF ENERGY, PASSION, AND DREAMS

You can apply all you've learned throughout this book, but you can be stopped in your tracks from making progress if you have **unforgiveness** in your heart. This may seem like a peculiar subject for a book on "Reframing and Rewiring." However, learning to forgive could be the most important step in your journey. In fact, if you've struggled in the past with overcoming certain obstacles or felt frustrated that you cannot make progress, this chapter could change everything for you!

First, let me make something clear. Forgiving a wrong does not mean that you forget or that the offender is absolved of the offense. Wrong is wrong, and the pain you suffered is real. Additionally, the choice to forgive is yours in the end. I hope you will take the time to read this chapter all the way through before making any decisions. Choosing to forgive is more about releasing you than it is about releasing the other person/s.

Ask yourself a few questions and try to be objective with your responses:

By choosing not to forgive . . .

- Are you suffering emotionally, mentally, or physically?
- Are you resolving the issue and making life better or bitter?
- Is it possible that you're damaging your relationships, due to anxiety or bitterness?
- Could you be missing out on opportunities in life or your career, due to your state of mind and/or health conditions brought on by your unforgiveness?
- Could you be creating neural networks that are eroding your perceptions on marriage, family, jobs, politics, religion, social interaction, investments, education, confidence, and other areas?
- Finally, do you think the offender is likely lying awake at night, unable to sleep, and feeling tormented because you don't forgive them? (Not likely)

Let's dive into a few real consequences of choosing not to forgive, beginning with your mental and physical health:

SIX EMOTIONAL EFFECTS OF BITTERNESS (UNFORGIVENESS)[15]

1. Prolonged Mental and Emotional Pain
2. Anxiety and/or Depression
3. Vindictive Behaviors
4. Distrust
5. Cynicism and Pessimism
6. Futility and Unhappiness

SIX PHYSICAL EFFECTS OF BITTERNESS (UNFORGIVENESS)

1. Insomnia
2. Hypertension
3. Back Pain
4. Headaches
5. Abdominal Conditions
6. Unhealthy Immune System

In 2010, Dr. Michael Barry wrote in his book *The Forgiveness Project* that 61 percent of cancer patients have forgiveness issues and, of those, more than half are severe. He also stated, "Harboring these negative emotions, this anger and hatred, creates a state of chronic anxiety."[16]

"Refusing to forgive makes people sick and keeps them that way."
—Dr. Steven Standiford, Chief of Surgery Cancer Treatment Centers of America

CASE STUDY #6
DEBORAH'S STORY

Anxiety and depression were not strangers to Deborah. She'd struggled with serious issues for over a decade. Like many of us, she came face-to-face with situations and circumstances she didn't know how to deal with early in life. She gave each challenge her best and tried to make sense of what was happening, often overthinking each wound. Deborah developed a habit of trying too hard to make things "right" and to make others happy, but her efforts never seemed to work. Eventually, the chaos drove her to a place of deep dissatisfaction, not only with the outcomes of each life challenge, but with herself. Even today, Deborah carries a strong desire to be excellent in every way.

In her attempts to gain relief, she tried a multitude of treatments, counselors, and therapists. All of her attempts to resolve her issues availed little, if any, results. At times, hopelessness overwhelmed her.

Deborah had a decent career, a husband who loved her, and children she cherished. However, the black cloud that constantly hung over her life was unbearable. It had been so long since she'd felt "normal" about her problems that she'd forgotten what normal was like.

The fact that things were "not really as bad as they could be" only made her feel worse about her depression because she couldn't shake off the disappointment she had in herself. She was unable to forgive herself for the way she was processing life. Her downward spiral had been out of control for so long that Deborah had completely lost her way.

The company where she worked was holding their annual all-staff training day, and I was the lunch keynote. The topic was Communicating with Resilience Under Pressure. For the first time in her life, Deborah had the opportunity to learn the science behind thoughts and how stress can alter our physiology. She became intrigued with this possibility, so she followed up after the training.

Our first discussion revealed her brokenness and desire to break free from the crippling effects of depression. However, Deborah was very reluctant to commit, since nothing had worked for her in the past.

Time passed, and Deborah contacted me again. She realized she needed to try something different, so she took the leap this time and began her new journey.

She wrote out her personal vision statement and determined which goals would be most helpful to her, personally and professionally. For five weeks, she filled her mind with powerful and insightful teaching through podcasts, audiobooks, quotes, articles, gratitude lists, and other resources. Each day she wrote down her thoughts and tracked her progress.

Deborah was learning to fill her daily schedule with positive, forward-thinking, intentional information that pushed her toward her vision. With each passing day, maintaining her routine became easier and more fluid. She also worked on adopting important habits to assist her in a complete routine makeover. She began exercising as often as she could, if only for 15 or 20 minutes at a time. She also began visualizing and taking time out for herself and her family. In addition, she was becoming increasingly aware of her ability to empower people in her world by spreading joy and kindness. The more Deborah stepped out of her past and into her future, the more hope arose in her. After about 3 weeks, she noticed dramatic changes in her physiology. She found herself smiling more, celebrating the small things, and enjoying life. She was finding new energy and was excited about where her journey was taking her.

After six weeks, Deborah had made so much progress that it became evident to her supervisor, her family members, and everyone close to her—so evident that they called to thank me and offered to buy more coaching for her so she could continue her journey out of darkness.

"Thank you for giving me my daughter back."
—Deborah's mom

Please note: Reframing and rewiring is not a cure for all cases of depression; however, our thoughts powerfully contribute to the composition of chemicals required to keep our mind and body in balance. Deborah will have to keep up her new daily routine long-term in order to completely recover. She did not become trapped by her condition overnight, and she will not reverse its effects overnight. However, she now has hope and the tools she needs to continue her journey to recovery.

Says Caroline Leaf, "Thoughts are real, physical things that occupy mental real estate. Moment by moment, every day, you are changing the structure of your brain through your thinking. When we hope, it is an activity of the mind that changes the structure of our brain in a positive and normal direction."[17]

THE 4-STEP JOURNEY TO FORGIVENESS

Forgiveness is rarely an event but, instead, a process or journey. As stated at the beginning of this chapter, the pain we feel from betrayal, suffering, or loss is very real and can take time to work through. Forgiving a wrong does not mean we declare that what happened to us is okay. Nor does it require us to pretend we don't remember the offense. In some cases, the offender is no longer with us or we are unable to communicate with them directly. Regardless of your current relationship with your offender, the choice to forgive is extremely important to *you*!

We receive multiple benefits when we choose to work through the process to forgive. Here are just a few:

- As long as we allow an offense to bind us in unforgiveness, we are shackled to our offender and, ultimately, to our past. Forgiving sets us free from those chains so we can find freedom for ourselves.
- When we forgive, over time we alter our body chemistry, or physiology, in both our bodies and minds. This increases our energy, calms our senses, and restores our health.
- We rediscover our lives, our happiness slowly returns, and our state of mind improves.

Follow the steps below, working through them every day for as long as it takes:

STEP #1: IDENTIFY THE HURT OR OFFENSE.

Label the offense *and* the feelings you may have as a result. Be as specific as you can. Consider writing them down on a sheet of paper and then destroying it or burying it as a way of symbolically declaring an "end" to your suffering.

- Who or what caused this offense?
- What was the offense?
- How did you feel at the time?
- How do you feel now?

STEP #2: CONFESS ANY HATRED YOU MAY HAVE.

It's not wrong to hate what happened or caused your offense. However, what you do about the hate will determine the outcome in your life. Here are some considerations:

- Projecting hatred inward, stuffing it down, or harboring a grudge wreaks havoc on our physical and mental health, our emotions, and our ability to function, ultimately leading to disease, depression, and other issues.

- Projecting hatred outwardly will likely destroy our healthy relationships, inflict harm upon the world around us, and diminish our personal and professional performance. Taking out hatred on an offender will never solve the issue. It will only increase our frustration and potentially harm our future.
- Deciding to hate **the offense itself,** rather than the offender (the "sin instead of the sinner"), is the healthiest direction to take in the first stages of forgiveness. Determine in your emotions and will that you will despise the offense and release the offender.

STEP #3: ACKNOWLEDGE AND RELINQUISH CONTROL.

Refusing to forgive provides a feeling of control or power over the offender, but the reality is that we cannot control others. In most cases, the offender is unaffected by our decision to hold them captive by our unforgiveness. Our feelings of control are a mask that covers our true feelings. Make the following declarations every day:

- I refuse to be a victim!
- I choose to cancel a debt I cannot collect.
- I make the decision to be free and move forward.
- I allow God, karma, or the Universe to be my vindicator and bring justice.
- I sever all ties and relinquish all control between myself and the offender.

STEP #4: ALLOW HEALING AND RESTORATION INTO YOUR HEART AND MIND.

Day by day, make the above declarations and choose a path of healing, allowing your heart and mind to be filled with thoughts of love and compassion for yourself.

Take time to pamper and express love, appreciation, and rejuvenation for yourself with walks in the park, long baths, hanging out with a friend, exercising, shooting some hoops, or anything that gives you a sense of wholeness and well-being. Each time you do this, meditate on your wholeness and happiness.

Speak the following affirmations over yourself to aid in this stage of forgiveness:

- I am calm, secure, and hopeful.
- I am filled with joy and strength.
- I am an overcomer in all things.
- I am blessed and valuable.
- I am talented and highly favored.
- I live each day with anticipation for a new life.

Allow yourself time, and feel free to express emotions as you work through this process. Cry, shout, vent, and share your experience with someone you trust. Even in moments of solitude, talking about your experience can be therapeutic. Prayers, journaling, and meditation are also effective in helping you sort out your feelings and detaching from the offense, as long as your goal is to reach the other side.

There is a Step #5 if you would like to take this to an even higher level. Consider writing a letter forgiving the offender and sending it to them or telling them you forgive them. You can also pray for them, speak blessings over them, or give them a gift of peace. This action is a bold step that can bring incredible restoration and a sense of completeness. Additionally, if you believe in reaping and sowing or karma, this action can change your destiny and open up amazing new opportunities.

As you apply each step and time passes, the offense will diminish, and your freedom will become evident, resulting in a magnificent future far beyond the place you once stood as new doors open for you.

SIXTH ASSIGNMENT

1. Consider anyone in your life, past or present, against whom you
    may be holding a grudge. This person could even be yourself.
    Write their names below:

    1. _____

    2. _____

    3. _____

    4. _____

    5. _____

> ### REFRAME AND REWIRE TIP #6
> Taking revenge or holding a grudge is like pouring a glass of
> poison for an offender and drinking it yourself.

ROUTINE BUILDERS FROM CHAPTER SIX

1. Forgiving a wrong does not mean we are declaring that what
    happened to us is okay. Nor does it require us to pretend we
    don't remember the offense.

    Beginning with each name, work through the 4 Steps to
    Forgiveness exercise in this chapter. Take as much time as you
    need with each name, but determine to stick with it until you
    forgive every name on your list.

GREATNESS TIP 6

Assignment #6 regarding forgiveness could be one of the hardest
tasks you have ever completed, but the freedom you receive when
you finish this portion of the journey will thrust you forward as if
a dam has broken and water that has long been held back is finally
free to flow.

CHAPTER SEVEN

GETTING "UNSTUCK" IN YOUR MIND AND HEART

I n the last chapter, we covered forgiveness of an offense. Hopefully, you've released this portion of your heart that's restrained you from moving forward so you can take one more step into your destiny.

Another important part of forgiveness can be holding your heart captive. Withholding self-forgiveness opposes the efforts you make to raise your standards, and it may be more difficult to relinquish than the previous step. This part of forgiveness requires letting go of the past.

Each of us has developed regret, remorse, or anger toward ourselves in our personal lives or careers. These feelings are sometimes caused by an experience or experiences we feel we "allowed" to happen to us, even if we were ignorant or helpless at the time. The circumstances could be partially our fault, or the events could be something we had no control over. We may have tried to "fix" or "save" the situation, but for whatever reason, we failed and lost something or someone valuable—perhaps some part of ourselves. Whatever the case may be, choosing to live in the past or dwell on a loss is the worst kind of unforgiveness—unforgiveness for ourselves. Remaining in this state chains us to our past and prevents us from moving forward.

In Chapter Two, you learned about the importance of having a VISION, and your assignment was to write your own personal Vision Statement. This step was intended to help you focus forward, rather than backward. Yet, if you do not deal with regrets or remorse about things in your past, you will be trapped in cognitive dissonance. When you are in a state of dissonance, every affirmation, new thought, or action becomes null and void. This happens because, when your Vision Statement stirs into reality in your mind and your heart brings it alive, every negative experience you recall or rehearse blasts your new neural networks with toxic, negative messages that send you in the opposite direction of your vision.

In other words, each time you react according to past experiences, rather than adhering to your new thought, life, and vision for the future, you send electrical impulses into old neural pathways and strengthen their connectivity. This habit *sustains old mindsets*, allowing them to remain dominant because they have deeper and wider connections than new ones.

Here are seven questions to ask yourself about past and potentially destructive thinking patterns:

- Were you told by someone you trusted, admired, or depended on that you were "no good," or "stupid," or perhaps something similar?
- Did you ever struggle with a subject, relationship, or job where you failed time and time again, making you feel like a failure and convincing you that you were "not good" at something? Or perhaps that you were "no good"?

- Have you ever tried to succeed at something you were passionate about, but the circumstances at the time prevented you from succeeding, and you became convinced that it wasn't a good idea for you to try again?
- Did you experience broken trust in your life or career, when someone seriously let you down, hurt you, or devastated you, making you feel that you could never trust again that way?
- Was there ever an occasion where you tried very hard to impress, and no matter what you did, it was never enough? Did the pain of rejection cause you to decide that it wasn't worth trying again?
- Did something catastrophic happen to you in your life or career that made you feel hopeless, lost, or uncertain about yourself, your future, and/or your abilities?
- Have you ever lost someone or something in your life or career that made you feel it was your fault, and you've been blaming yourself ever since that time?

SEVENTH ASSIGNMENT

Check the box for each of the seven questions that pertain to you personally. Pull yourself out of your skin (disconnect from your emotions), and objectively think about whether your beliefs are true.

If you find yourself feeling "stuck" again and again trying to form long-lasting relationships, solid business plans, successful endeavors, or just feeling good about yourself, then read on . . . this chapter is for YOU!

Below are four lies we commonly buy into. They are formative mindsets that keep us "stuck" and unable to move forward into greatness:

LIES WE BELIEVE ABOUT OURSELVES:

Perhaps you've bought into a lie you believed about yourself or were told by someone you looked up to. If we're honest and are willing to work at altering our perceptions through cognitive transformation, we may discover that the lies we've accepted as truth for so long can no longer control us.

> *"Other people's opinions of you do not*
> *have to become your reality."*
> —Les Brown

WALLS WE BUILD AROUND OURSELVES:

Hurts, disappointment, and rejection are all very real and very painful. Unknowingly, we may build walls around ourselves to prevent these things from happening again. We can justify this as being wise or cautious. But because we often rehearse the incident so much, it can become over-inflated to the point that the memory shuts us down.

Ultimately, we want to build a strong neural network that affects us in healthy ways in all of our relationships. Through a commitment to brain training, we can restore healthy mindsets over time and raise our emotional and social intelligence.

INNER VOWS:

When we encounter situations, events, or circumstances where we find ourselves backed against a wall or strongly opposed to what is happening, we may unknowingly create "Inner Vows." I knew someone who made an inner vow concerning soda pop. He grew up restricted from drinking soda pop by his parents. The day he moved out as an adult, he filled his closet with soda pop and became almost pushy about offering it to any guest who visited his apartment. Additionally, he drank it with every meal, despite its unhealthy consequences.

I could use other examples, but I hope this one helps you see where you may have made your own inner vows.

FEAR OF FAILURE:

Inevitably, all of us will fail throughout our lives. This is not a news flash for any of us. However, there are times when a failure can trap us, destroying our potential and discouraging us from pushing through into success. In fact, when we perceive a failure wrongly, it resonates with us like rejection, causing us to rehearse it over and over. Instead of failure becoming the foundation for growth and learning, it becomes a stumbling block that trips us up and damages us for life. When we determine that we are unable or ill-equipped, we sell ourselves short and stunt our opportunity for advancement in life and career.

Despite your setbacks, you have what it takes to reframe and rewire! You CAN create a new you, a new destiny, and open the doors to new opportunities. Give yourself permission to forgive anything in your past that may have created success-inhibiting mind blocks. Decide to let the past be the past. You must do this in order to achieve a fixed and solid focus on your future. Only then can you establish a mindset that will make your affirmations powerful and create cognitive consonance. You will experience a clear, peaceful, and stable state of mind that will propel you into amazing realities you never thought possible. This freedom is required if you want to continue to crush bad habits for radical change.

Listed below are names you may recognize as people who did not allow damaging remarks, failures, struggles, or deceptions from their past get in the way of winning: [18]

Thomas Edison was told he was "too stupid to learn" by his teacher, and he was fired by his first employers for being "unproductive." He even failed 1,000 times at perfecting the lightbulb. Still, his determined spirit responded, *"I didn't fail 1,000 times, the light bulb was an invention with 1,000 steps."*

Henry Ford failed and went broke five times before he succeeded at inventing the Ford motor car.

Michael Jordan stated, "I've missed more than 9000 shots in my career. I've lost almost 300 games; 26 times, I've been trusted to take the game-winning shot . . . and missed. I've failed over and over and over again in my life. That is why I succeed."

Walt Disney was fired, went bankrupt, and was rejected. A newspaper editor said, "He lacked imagination and had no good ideas." The city of Anaheim told him he'd only attract lowlifes to the amusement park the world now knows as Disneyland.

Lucille Ball began studying to be an actress in 1927. The head instructor of the John Murray Anderson Drama School told her to "try any other profession," but those words did not stop her.

Colonel Sanders started his endeavors to begin a successful fried chicken restaurant at 65 and failed 1009 times before succeeding. Whether you like KFC or not, the story of Colonel Harland Sanders is truly amazing. He has become a renowned figure by marketing his "finger lickin' good" Kentucky Fried Chicken.[19]

CASE STUDY #7
SOPHIA'S STORY

This story is unique, as it begins with a list of setbacks and unfortunate circumstances, personally and professionally. However, due to Sophia's application of many practices shared in this book, she created a dynamic new daily routine for herself that ultimately turned around many circumstances for her at multiple levels.

The story begins after a 4-year streak of life-altering challenges for Sophia and her family, including:

- Job loss from company downsizing
- Serious injury, leaving her unable to walk for nine months and unable to drive for many of those months
- A failed business venture
- Another job loss from a business closing
- Yes, one more job loss from a company closing its United States office
- A house with ongoing structural issues, despite repairs and complete replacement of multiple areas
- House flooding that destroyed the main level, and insurance that didn't cover ground water flooding
- Husband's unexpected, life-threatening health issue and an injury resulting in complete loss of income for more than 12 months. This was in addition to her own income loss.
- A plethora of uninsured medical expenses
- Eventual home foreclosure

All of the above happened immediately after the loss of Sophia's financial resources, when a dishonest investment company dissolved the family business shortly after taking all of Sophia's savings and investment funds.

To top it off, her favorite dog died. Sophia's life was like a bad country song!

In the midst of all of this, she fought hard to keep her head above water. She willingly worked every job, even those that she never imagined she would settle for. Her earnings were a fraction of the pay rate she'd previously earned. She was downtrodden, guilt-ridden, and exasperated by the flood of failures and difficult circumstances. Despite her efforts or prior achievements, all seemed hopeless. Nevertheless, amidst the chaos, Sophia remained determined not to give up. It was during this time that she reached out to me.

Soon after we met, Sophia began a daily routine of encouragement, including motivational videos for morning inspiration and audio books for personal development. She also worked hard on a daily affirmation program. Her pursuits for knowledge and changes in her mindsets included in-depth research of many helpful topics that fascinated and empowered her. Topics such as:

- Effective personal affirmations
- Visualization techniques
- Epigenetics
- Neuroscience
- Quantum physics

Being of Christian faith, she was especially intrigued about the way the topics she was studying aligned with instructions given in the Bible for life, success, and happiness.

Sophia continued on this new path of learning while continuing to grow and retrain her brain. She was excited about her vision of complete restoration. She believed she would gain back far more than she had lost. She even wrote down a list of specific things she wanted to see and continued to work on believing, speaking, and pursuing. Her focus and conversation shifted from complaining and worrying about things she could not control to talking about things she believed in her heart would truly happen.

A new home was one of the goals high on her list. After she wrote down every detail of what she wanted in a home, she began searching for something that fit that description. Sophia diligently spent every spare moment looking at as many homes as possible. Keep in mind that she had no money, no credit, and no equity in the home she was losing and had limited time with the bank to get out of her current home.

The second thing on Sophia's "critical needs" list was a job. She had become very good at job-hunting, but this time she came at her job search with a strong belief that she would obtain the right job. Interestingly, a position materialized for her. During introductions in her first week at work, she discovered that this employer shared many of her same Christian values. When her co-workers asked if they could pray for her, one of them shared that Sophia was praying for a home closer to work. As the prayers and conversations continued, another co-worker spoke up and asked, "You don't happen to want a lake house, do you?"

This was a shock to her, because a lake house was exactly what she had written on her list and had been visualizing. Upon receiving more details, she discovered it could be a "rent to own" opportunity. This could not have been a better setup for her, considering her financial circumstances. All of this happened within the timeframe she needed in order to meet the deadline on the foreclosure.

Below is the exact list of affirmations Sophia wrote and sent to me, detailing the home she was visualizing. It includes her check marks and notes describing the fulfillment of each one on the list:

- I'm going to have a house on a lake—on one of the top two lakes I'd been searching!
- I'd like it to have just two bedrooms so it's less work to maintain. Got it!
- I don't want a lot of stairs to get into the house. It had a ramp!
- I really want the laundry on the main level. Got it!
- Even though I only need 2 bedrooms, I still want a 2nd bathroom. It has 2 full bathrooms!
- I want the yard to have a gradual decline from the house to the water, so it's not uncomfortably steep to walk down, but also not in danger of flooding. Perfectly gradual!

- It has to have a sandy bottom waterfront, where I can walk in gradually without slime or swampy muck or weed. Pristine sand!
- It has to have a lot of large windows overlooking the water. The entire waterfront is a wall of floor-to-ceiling windows!
- The lake has to be deep enough to have the right kind of fish that my husband likes to fish for. Perch and walleye included!
- It has to be an all-sports lake so we can boat, once we get a boat. Got it!
- It still needs to be relatively peaceful on the water and with generous distance in proximity to neighbors. It's on a dead-end road and the neighbors are seasonal. They are rarely there!
- I joked that I didn't care if the house had ugly wallpaper. Well, let's just say, it's not my style.
- I also said I didn't even care if the lake house had an ugly kitchen. (I was a bit sad about giving up the new kitchen we'd purchased and had installed in the old house.) The kitchen was so ugly! Ha-ha! . . . with lots of great storage, though!

Amazingly, the lake property was worth more than double the value of the home Sophia lost. She was very thankful and excited for what was next in her life. In her own words, she stated, "It has only just begun!"

The following are words she wrote as a testimonial for this book:

Michelle dragged me out of my hopelessness when I had become too exhausted by my circumstances to push forward on my own. She reached out with her hand of inspiration to lift me up and push me forward, motivating me into the truth of my purpose. She was the only one. Everyone else tried to limit me within my circumstances. More than ever, I was tempted to limit myself. I am so grateful for the tools she shared with me. These intentional practices truly change everything.

"Don't worry about failures, worry about the chances
you miss when you don't even try."
—Jack Canfield, *Chicken Soup for the Soul*

As crazy as it sounds, one of the things I had to learn years ago was to expect trials and adversities, rather than trying to dodge them. Not that I focused ON them or visualized them, because that would be counterproductive, and it would contradict everything I have been sharing in this book.

Instead, I came to the realization that tough times, failures, and challenges are unavoidable. Living life hoping they won't happen is a false pretense and will always catch us unprepared. When we live with this mindset, we set ourselves up to be overtaken by life's challenges. We develop reactive thinking. This type of thinking sets off a downward spiral of disappointment, hurt, anger, and a victim's mentality. This reactive response inevitably leads us into depression, disease, and both mental and physical illness.

Think about the word "dis-ease." Although the common definition means illness, the origin of the word is French, meaning "lack of ease." This can be correlated with many of the things we have already discussed, like cognitive dissonance, unforgiveness, lack of confidence, offense, and other issues.

Allowing reactive thinking in our lives places us in old mindsets and sets us up for disaster. When we react, our electrical impulses fire through past neural networks that may be on the brink of becoming obsolete in areas where we are working to retrain our brain. This revives old habits by breathing new life into them and, ultimately, resurrecting these old habits.

Each time we succumb to old patterns, the neurosynaptic response triggers a release of toxic hormones all over again, and we re-establish old routines, leading us right back to disease, depression, and toxic living, etc. The only way to avoid this vicious cycle is to maintain a consistent and powerful daily routine.

Just as Sophia did, you must resolve to rise every day and make a choice to bolster your mind and heart by filling them with the right kind of information. Empower yourself with thoughts and feelings that equip you to stand strong against things that may distract or discourage you. At the same time, maintain a mindset of expectation for good things to happen, and get serious about your destiny!

REFRAME AND REWIRE TIP #7
Living where you are and focusing *forward* rather than *backward* takes time, practice, and determination. This discipline can be compared to driving forward while looking through the rearview mirror, instead of the windshield.

ROUTINE BUILDERS FROM CHAPTER SEVEN

1. Go back and reread the four reactive mindsets we tend to form in our lifetime. For each one, describe areas where this may have happened to you. Then write a counter thought or affirmation you can use to reverse the negative effects in your life and/or career:

LIES WE BELIEVE ABOUT OURSELVES

_____
_____
_____
_____
_____
_____

WALLS WE BUILD AROUND OURSELVES

_____

_____

_____

_____

_____

_____

INNER VOWS

_____

_____

_____

_____

_____

_____

FEAR OF FAILURE

_____

_____

_____

_____

_____

_____

GREATNESS TIP 7

Realize that everyone has or will face adversity. You are not alone. The difference between being overcome by adversity and moving forward is to choose how you will process challenges every day.

GREATNESS TIP 8

Having a written "Vision Statement" is not enough. We must constantly and consistently keep it in front of us and use it in every area of life.

PART TWO

MASTERING HABITS AND CREATING A ROUTINE FOR SUCCESS

CHAPTER EIGHT

PLAYERS, ENERGY, AND VAMPIRES

In the first section of this book, we dealt with multiple layers of heart, mind, and physiological issues that prevent us from making progress in our journey to reframe and rewire. This next section is filled with ideas, tips, and tricks to aid us on our journey. Before we dive in, it's important to remind you of two essential concepts:

CONCEPT ONE

As mentioned in the beginning, this process is a journey. That means that everything you apply must become a lifestyle. You must adopt a brand-new way of seeing and thinking when you rise, prepare for your day, and deal with the tasks and challenges in front of you. This takes time, study, practice, and effort. There is no "secret formula" to reaching greatness. The small changes you make over time progressively alter how you view your life and career, as well as how you respond to it. No one can read this book, or any book, just once and suddenly be transformed into the person they wish to become. We must commit to reading, rereading, applying, and growing—consistently and unceasingly.

If you understand and have applied what you've read in the first seven chapters, you should be seeing yourself and the world around you differently. The key is implementing what you've learned and practiced with an ongoing commitment to change.

CONCEPT TWO

It is absolutely vital that you deal with your mind and heart before any of the next chapters can have a significant effect on you. The "soil of your subconscious" cannot retain good seed, nor can it produce a bountiful harvest if it is tainted by hurt, bitterness, hatred, offense, and negativity. Reading or studying self-help books or materials to improve your life or career will simply dissipate or quickly be forgotten because you have not altered your "inner life" in order to receive these truths.

As written in earlier chapters, the process of creating new neural pathways begins with the growth of new dendrites. Just like a newborn baby needs constant attention and nourishment, newly formed and growing neural networks need attention and nourishment. If they do not receive attention at least every 48 hours, they can denature, or turn into hot air. How many times have you learned or read something that influenced you, but it ultimately did not change you? This is because you did not attend to your mind and heart by creating new habits and routines to incorporate the change.

I am reminded of an analogy/parable found in three of the Synoptic Gospels in the Christian Bible (Matthew, Mark, and Luke) and the Arabic Life of Buddha. Aside from the suppositions of "religion," the wisdom in this story helps explain the significance of this important understanding. Its relevance is clearly universal, despite its origin.

The first parable as written in the book of Matthew (the first of four Gospels) in chapter 13 of the Christian Bible:

A farmer went out to sow his seed. As he was scattering the seed, some fell along the path, and the birds came and ate it up. Some fell on rocky places, where it did not have much soil. It sprang up quickly, because the soil was shallow. But when the sun came up, the plants were scorched, and they withered because they had no root. Other seed fell among thorns, which grew up and choked the plants. Still other seed fell on good soil, where it produced a crop—a hundred, sixty or thirty times what was sown.

—Matthew 13:3–9 (NKJV)

The second is a quote from "The Arabic Life of Buddha," Bilauhar and Budasaf's version of the parable of the sower. In fact, it is almost identical to the one written above:

The sower is the bearer of wisdom. The good seed is the good word. That which falls on the wayside and the birds steal is that which is only just heard, and then forgotten. That which falls on the rocky ground, which is wet and then dry when roots reach the rock, that's the listener who is good for a moment, when he hears it and his heart is ready, and it seizes his intelligence, but he does not hold it in his memory, his intention or his reason. That which grows and gets to the point of giving fruit, but thorns make it perish, is that which the listener retains and understands, but when it comes time for action, which is the fruit, lusts stifle it and make it perish. Finally, that which falls on good ground and remains intact, grows, matures and prospers is that which the eye perceives, the ear retains, the heart preserves, and is put into practice with firm resolution, following the act of taming lusts and purifying the heart of defilement.[20]

Despite being deemed as religious in nature, this basic truth can be found in many other readings or philosophies. Interestingly, it describes the process of neuroplasticity in an accurate but parabolic way.

The birds and the rocky soil represent our hearts in a hardened state, when we're unable to grasp or hold onto new concepts due to hurt, deception, and other impediments discussed in previous chapters. The new growth of dendrites does not thrive amid these impediments as it does in good soil. Therefore, new growth squelched or simply converts into hot air within a couple of days.

The description of the seeds sown in weedy, thorny soil portrays an analogy about what happens to newly formed neural pathways as a result of retraining or rewiring our brains. Despite the value we may find in new concepts, we reason using old, familiar thinking patterns based on our go-to negative emotions. Just as plants become choked out, our thoughts become consumed by the cares of this world, depriving new pathways of the necessary electricity needed to thrive, and, therefore, they denature.

Finally, the good soil, which retains seeds and consistently nourishes them, produces extended periods of consistent growth, which multiplies the plants. The same is true with creating new neural networks. In time, new growth increases the power to multiply our perceptions and can even change characteristics of our personality. Ultimately, we alter our subconscious, thereby creating a new future.

The unfortunate truth is that the process can occur within us in either a positive or a negative manner.

THREE MAJOR PLAYERS IN ESTABLISHING GREATNESS

Greatness is more about WHO you are than WHAT you do. The three major players we will discuss in the next chapters are crucial in learning how to consistently reframe and rewire.

ENERGY—FOCUS—TIME

ENERGY: When we have the energy and desire to establish a new daily routine, we must also develop focus and make time in order to be successful. Like a three-legged stool, the three concepts work together. Energy requires our commitment to health, exercise, rest, proper nutrition, and self-care. We must also feed and refresh our spirit and soul with positive, energizing, regenerative messages.

FOCUS: Having the ability to FOCUS and work through tasks undistracted is good. However, we must focus on motivating and energizing ourselves so we don't grow weary and lose interest. Focus means carefully planning what we do each day to create a well-managed daily routine.

TIME: When we incorporate excellent planning and time management to accomplish our priorities, we're certain to make progress. Our success relies upon our ability to consistently generate the right energy while maintaining laser-like focus.

We must equally balance all three areas in order to triumph over old habits, tendencies, and patterns that have defeated us in the past. The remainder of this chapter and subsequent chapters are devoted to the three components above. There are also plenty of tools, hacks, and insights to help you establish the best routine for you.

ENERGY VAMPIRES

According to a study of 540 business leaders by Fast Company:[21]

- 82 percent were found to be not working at optimal energy levels
- 61 percent recognized that they were working well below their best energy levels
- 21 percent stated that they were working above their best energy levels

"Energy reflects performance."
—Theresa Wellbourne, eePulse, Inc.

EIGHTH ASSIGNMENT

Take the brief energy quiz to find out how much you have. This quiz can also be downloaded and printed at:

reframeandrewire.com

ENERGY QUIZ

Energy and motivation are critical attributes to scoring high in Emotional Intelligence.

Take this simple quiz to discover how well you manage your energy and your influence.

Answer each question honestly, based on your beliefs and behaviors before reading this book. Answer T or F (True/False), then use the chart below to calculate your scores.

1. _____ On average, I need only 4–5 hours of sleep each night to function well.
2. _____ I consume half of my body weight (lbs.) in ounces of water each day.

3. _____ Fear is an effective way to motivate people.

4. _____ Disorganization and clutter make me mentally exhausted and less productive.

5. _____ Everyone is motivated by the same thing.

6. _____ Reading motivational books and listening to educational messages are a part of my daily routine.

7. _____ People who are motivated are typically more extroverted by nature.

8. _____ Encouraging others consistently only pampers them and is ineffective.

9. _____ Laughter helps with problem-solving and memory.

10. _____ I spend at least 60 minutes per day "unplugged" from tasks or devices.

11. _____ Eating healthy is great for the body but has little effect on the brain.

12. _____ Nuts and berries are energy boosting and a regular part of my diet.

13. _____ I believe in setting the bar unrealistically high for my team and myself.

14. _____ I have learned how to say "NO" out of respect for myself and my priorities.

15. _____ I exercise 35 times per week and notice a big difference when I don't.

16. _____ Our world is so full of negativism, it's impossible to avoid.

17. _____ Success means different things to different people.

18. _____ Personal organization can help us gain and sustain motivation.

19. _____ It is important to celebrate success for our teams and ourselves.

20. _____ I maintain an excellent state of mind, which empowers me, personally and professionally.

SCORING YOUR QUIZ

Circle and calculate your total points based on the answers below. Add all together and refer to the scoring results.

KEY: 1=Incorrect, 2=Correct

#	Points	#	Points	#	Points	#	Points
1	T = 1 F = 2	6	T = 2 F = 1	11	T = 1 F = 2	16	T = 1 F = 2
2	T = 2 F = 1	7	T = 1 F = 2	12	T = 2 F = 1	17	T = 2 F = 1
3	T = 1 F = 2	8	T = 1 F = 2	13	T = 1 F = 2	18	T = 2 F = 1
4	T = 2 F = 1	9	T = 2 F = 1	14	T = 2 F = 1	19	T = 2 F = 1
5	T = 1 F= 2	10	T = 2 F = 1	15	T = 2 F = 1	20	T = 2 F = 1

SCORE (TOTAL OF ALL ADDED) _____

TOTAL SCORE OF 36–40: You have a good understanding of what it takes to create self-motivation and daily energy. You are empowered and fully capable of taking on whatever challenges you may face with a positive outlook and powerful resolve. Work on the areas you marked incorrectly to take your energy to the next level.

TOTAL SCORE OF 32–35: You are on the right track and have a fairly good handle on what it takes to energize and motivate yourself. However, it will be important for you to overcome the areas where you scored a 1 if you desire to rise higher and accomplish more with unstoppable resolve.

TOTAL SCORE OF 20–31: You are most likely finding life and career a struggle. In fact, you may feel as if you are constantly exhausted. The first step for you is to realize that motivation and energy are primarily established by choice, lifestyle, and practice. These attributes are learned. They are not inherited or thrust upon us due to circumstances. This is demonstrated by many historical "greats" who overcame insurmountable odds. Be sure to do all the assignments in this book to increase your score.

IDENTIFYING ENERGY VAMPIRES

Your next steps will include studying about what it takes to motivate you, inspire you, and give you energy for each day. This means that you may need to give up "energy vampires" and take on new habits for your daily routine (energy boosters). Changes in diet, activity, thoughts, and mindsets are the only true and lasting solutions to this dilemma. If you desire more counsel or help, please visit *ipvconsulting.com.*

Energy Vampires are habits or actions that can drain your energy on a day-to-day basis. A few are listed below to help you adjust your new routine. As you read more about them, mark off the areas where you would like to improve.

Remember, the little things you do each day can make the biggest difference in your journey.

#1—LACK OF SLEEP

There are conflicting reports about the average amount of sleep an adult must have to function optimally. Many reports say 8 hours; others say between 6–8 hours. The point is, neglecting the amount of sleep needed for optimum functioning can severely affect our performance. In an article published in *Scientific American*, John Peever, Director of the Systems Neurobiology Lab at the University of Toronto, and Brian J Murray, Director of the Sleep Laboratory, Sunnybrook Health Sciences Center, agree about the value of sleep. "Sleep serves to reenergize the body's cells, clear waste from the brain and support learning and memory. It even plays vital roles in regulating mood, appetite and libido."[22]

Without adequate sleep cycles, we set ourselves up for brain fatigue, brain fog, anxiety, poor nutritional habits, illness, and several other disorders affecting our ability to function at our optimum.

#2—DEHYDRATION

According to multiple reports and government sources, approximately 75 percent of Americans may suffer from chronic dehydration.[23] Since dehydration is rarely recognized in most cases until it becomes severe, the majority of the population remains unconcerned and unresolved about this problem. Water is lost through normal daily bodily functions such as breathing, talking, and urinating. It is also lost through sweat and bowel movements. Dehydration occurs when a lack of hydrating beverages are being taken in, or too many non-hydrating beverages are consumed (i.e., caffeinated, alcoholic, or drinks high in sodium/sugar).

You should be drinking no less than half your body weight in ounces of water, daily. Example: 128 pounds in body weight would be 64 ounces of water per day.

When you are dehydrated, you will experience a reduction in blood volume and thickening of the blood, causing your heart to work harder and less efficiently. In addition, the circulation of oxygen and nutrients is minimized, reducing cell and chemical or hormone restoration. A few symptoms are headaches, fatigue, irritability, difficulty focusing, reduced metabolism, and many other success-crippling issues.

#3—LACK OF EXERCISE

Below are some remarkable statistics regarding the relationship of exercise to success. If you're already aware of these statistics and applying them consistently, I applaud you.

- Exercising just 20–30 minutes, 3–5 times per week can cause the pituitary gland to flood your body with endorphins, significantly reducing causes of depression while elevating moods. Other advantages are an invigorated immune system, expanded creativity, clarity of mind, improved learning potential, retention of information, along with many more benefits.

Several reports, including one by Stanford University and the *New York Times*, have indicated that endorphins are 200 times more powerful than morphine. They can act as painkillers! Some even describe the effects of endorphins as a euphoric feeling or "runner's high." [24]

- Regular exercise also reduces cortisol in the body and brain, often producing better sleep patterns and aiding in weight loss.
- Those who exercise regularly tend to have much higher energy levels and keener senses, including the ability to focus on projects for long periods of time without becoming fatigued.

Are you convinced yet? There are many other benefits but almost no consequences for the average individual. Even those with disabilities can find ways to exercise within their limitations.

Exercise does not have to be complicated or even cost a lot. For example, walking each day, taking the stairs, stretching, participating in floor exercises, or even heavy lifting are all valuable and practical.

Note: All exercise routines should be approached under the guidance of a physician, especially when health concerns or limitations exist.

#4—LACK OF UPLUGGING AND SOCIAL TIME

Recent studies have reported that US consumers spend approximately 4–5 hours per day on their cell phones. In fact, on average, cell phone users check their phones every 5–7 minutes. Often there is no real reason, other than habit. Added up over a lifetime, this calculates to approximately 6 years of time wasted on a device. Furthermore, if we add in television, our average tech time is approximately 7 years. The sum of these two is 13 years! [25]

These numbers are staggering and unacceptable.

Unless we are intentional, we will rarely get a break from the "blings and dings" of devices day and night. We must ask ourselves what this might be doing to us and to the generations after us.

The science behind device addictions has shown that notifications produce a small amount of dopamine each time they alert us, due to the reaction caused by someone liking our posts or sending us a private message. Dopamine even has the power to turn off certain receptor sites within the amygdala (the emotional center of the brain), reducing cortisol and stress. Though the effects are small, device addictions can lure us into conversations that may challenge us and possibly even enrage us. [26]

At the very least, devices steal away precious time we could be spending in more constructive ways.

Obviously, we could list other distractions, but devices are one of the biggest time drains in today's culture.

Some of the consequences of not unplugging are

- Risk of burnout
- Destruction of creativity

- Inhibitors of concentration and focus
- Resentment of jobs or other obligations
- Unhealthy device addiction
- Potential "fallout" in relationships
- Reduction in productivity
- "Blue light" effects, including insomnia

Addiction to devices has been on the rise over the past two decades. In 2017, Harvard Health Publishing released results of a "blue light" study in an article called "Blue Light has a Dark Side." The report found that when we spend too much time in front of blue lights (i.e., devices or LED lighting) or do so within 3 hours of bedtime, it disrupts our biological clock or circadian rhythm. This effect suppresses the secretion of melatonin (the hormone responsible in assisting us to sleep). Additional studies reveal that it may be a contributing cause of cancer, diabetes, heart disease, and obesity.[27] These studies are still in the early stages, but it is fair to argue that too much light exposure is having an effect on us.

I am not advocating that we destroy all of our devices or even ignore them, as I have plenty of my own. They do serve a purpose, just as dishwashers and other appliances do. It's a matter of learning how to take back control, placing priority on things that enrich our lives, rather than possess our lives.

Unplugging also entails finding time for yourself: time to be in the present, to reflect or meditate; time to work on your goals and your dreams; time to enjoy family and friends or to just be.

#5—CHRONIC STRESS

Since we covered the effects of chronic stress in earlier chapters, I will not go back through the details of what elevated cortisol can do to your brain and your health. However, *chronic stress* is included on this list because it is a major energy vampire. When we allow ourselves to remain in a state of stress or anxiety, we physically wear down faster than when we are only affected by physical exertion.

We were not designed to be under constant stress, and when we are, we destroy our ability to manage the three major players in establishing greatness.

ENERGY: Chronic stress makes it impossible for us to produce, due to the physiological impact of poor thinking, as well as physical and emotional exhaustion.

FOCUS: Chronic stress produces elevated amounts of cortisol that paralyze portions of our frontal cortex, causing fatigue and brain blocks. When we are under chronic stress, our ability to focus becomes impaired.

TIME: Chronic stress puts us under pressure, creating a lifestyle of reactivity, instead of proactivity. Our time management also becomes jeopardized, which creates a lifestyle of reactivity, instead of proactivity.

Other energy vampires to consider are:

- Disorganization or clutter
- Perfectionism
- Overthinking
- Negativity
- Trouble saying "no"
- Too much junk food or sugar
- Too much caffeine
- No clarity or written vision
- No written goals
- Fault-finding or cynicism

REFRAME AND REWIRE TIP #8
Every thought, action, or habit you choose either pushes you forward or holds you back. Create a daily routine that will align your mind, heart, and emotions with your purposes and intentions for a better future.

This is not an exhaustive list, but my hope is that you're beginning to pull the facts together and consider a routine that will empower you and help you live at a higher level.

ROUTINE BUILDERS FROM CHAPTER EIGHT

1. Consider each of the energy vampires listed in this chapter and check off the areas where you've developed consistent habits and patterns.

2. Now consider how you will counter each one by making specific changes in your daily routine. Remember, you cannot achieve changes overnight; you did not get where you are overnight. However, if you list your vampires below and develop a plan to work on a few at a time, you can make considerable progress in your growth into greatness.

_____
_____
_____
_____
_____
_____
_____
_____
_____
_____
_____
_____

CHAPTER NINE

INSANE FOCUS AND PRODUCTIVITY HACKS

As mentioned in the last chapter, the three most important skills for greatness are energy, focus, and time. Just as we created a plan of action for filling our hearts and minds with the right thoughts and influences, we must develop a plan of action for managing our time and focus. This chapter presents practical focus habits and productivity hacks to help you improve the task management portion of your new daily routine.

#1 BRAIN DUMP AND PRIORITIZE.

Nothing can drain you more than feeling overloaded with projects, obligations, tasks, and deadlines. You can be inundated with so much to accomplish that you feel suffocated and unable to accomplish your goals. I've encountered this personally, as well as with many of my clients.

The best solution is to develop the habit of taking five minutes to create two lists, one for professional tasks and one for personal tasks. Then "brain dump" every project that's on your mind onto the lists. You'll discover instant relief knowing everything is in writing.

The next step is to prioritize each list. You can do this with numbers or by highlighting in colors:

- PINK = Urgent
- YELLOW = Somewhat Urgent
- GREEN = Not Urgent

Stephen Covey writes about a phenomenal 4-quadrant system of prioritizing tasks in *The 7 Habits of Highly Effective People*.

The key to managing all big projects is to "chunk" them down into smaller increments of time, rather than allowing them to overwhelm us.

Once you've arranged both lists, work out a plan of action to complete the top five tasks. Schedule reasonable timeframes on your calendar, making sure that you're able to complete each item in the allotted period.

Break non-priority tasks into reasonable timeframes and assign deadlines for completion. For example, if you want to write a book, allocate the days of the week you can write and the timeframes during which you will write. Keep in mind that you must be consistent and committed to staying on track, or you will never complete your goals. Choose the mindset that these goals are just as important as your priority tasks, but with the understanding that deadlines can be extended as needed. When we take time to actually schedule out the tasks we must accomplish, we increase the likelihood of completing them.

Brain dumping and prioritizing are critical habits to develop and maintain for a lifetime and should be done every week or at least every month. This discipline empowers us to stay intentional and accomplish what we would otherwise never finish.

NINTH ASSIGNMENT

The next pages include a powerful 30-Day Goal Setting Planner with guidelines and instructions. A download is available at *reframeandrewire.com*. Take time to use this tool to create your first 30-day plan.

5-STEP PERFORMANCE GOALSETTING
(30-DAY PLANNER)

STEP 1—List 10 things you want to achieve for your business/career/life in the next 30 days (print this page every month, re-examine, and re-write your goals).

STEP 2—Prioritize these goals in an order that will influence your life/career to the greatest measure. Use the second column provided to change the order of numbers in order of priority.

1		
2		
3		
4		
5		
6		
7		
8		
9		
10		

STEP 3—Begin with the Top 3 Goals and work your way through.

What **RESOURCES** will you need?	Who do you need to **CONNECT** with?
What **EDUCATION** will you need to pursue?	What **OBSTACLES** will you encounter?

STEP 4—Break down the required steps by weekly and daily task lists. **Print additional copies of this page to use EVERY WEEK.**

What must I work on this week to move forward in accomplishing my goals?

Step 5—What TASKS must I complete each DAY to fulfill the work listed above and reach my listed goals?

MONDAY	
TUESDAY	
WEDNESDAY	
THURSDAY	
FRIDAY	
WEEKEND TASKS	

#2 PREP FOR THE WEEK AND THEN FOR THE DAY.

The majority of the working population wastes 60–90 minutes at the beginning of each day trying to acclimate, prepare, and determine where to begin our work projects. We often begin with email, social media, chatting with co-workers, and other time wasters. Then, at the close of the day or the week, we complain about our inability to keep up with projects and the demands of our jobs.

Ultimately, this kind of routine only puts more stress on us and deprives us of quality time at home because we haven't accomplished enough during our workday. As a result, we can wind up in a downward spiral of frustration, remorse, oppression, lack of peace, and sleeplessness.

The remedy is simple.

While our work week is still fresh in our minds, take 15–20 minutes at the close of every week to write down the projects or issues we must address on Monday morning, place them in priority order, and set up corresponding appointments or calls. Then take 5 minutes at the close of each day of the week (Monday–Thursday), and write out a prioritized list for the beginning of the next day.

A great way to approach this habit is to go through emails and clear our desk. I find this practice effective in helping me create a priority list, but it also dramatically improves the organization of my workspace.

This 20–30 minute at the end of the week helps us stay on task, close out our work week with far less stress, and unplug at home, knowing we put into writing everything we need to begin the next day/week.

#3 WEAPONS OF MASS DISTRACTION

The brain is not equipped to provide clear, creative focus when it's distracted by people, calls, notifications, and other interruptions. Distractions can seriously infringe upon our creativity and ability to accomplish projects that require our full attention. In fact, when there are too many distractions, the resulting distraction can produce multiple, even detrimental mistakes that compounds our workload, our frustration, and our likelihood of making errors.

In Chapter Eight, we covered Energy Vampire #4. Studies show that the average individual checks their phone approximately every 5–7 minutes, even when there are no notifications. Checking our phones has become a habit. In fact, experts now equate the dings and blings of notifications to be similar to cocaine addiction urges.[28]

Here are a few more statistics on this topic as it relates to the topics of focus and time:

According to an article published on Adweek.com in 2017, statistics showed that we spend an average of 2 hours per day on social media platforms:[29]

- 40 minutes on YouTube
- 35 minutes on Facebook
- 25 minutes on Snapchat
- 15 minutes on Instagram
- 1 minute on Twitter

If you add this up, our tech time comes out to an average lifetime total of 5 years and 4 months. Add in the addiction of television with the average lifetime total of 7 years and 8 months, and **the final number of time lost is 13 years and 2 months**. These are years we could spend with those we love or investing in bettering ourselves.

Time is the most precious commodity we have, and it is one commodity that cannot be bought back or renewed.

The solution is to become INTENTIONAL every day by using the following tips:

- When you're working on projects, meeting with people, spending time with family, or just unplugging, shut off all notifications and alerts on your devices. Set "check times" for looking at your emails, social media notifications, texts, voicemails, etc. Example: 10am, 12pm, 2pm, 5pm, and 8pm.
- Devices are created to serve us; this practice should never be the other way around. The more intentional you become about scheduling times to check messages, the less likely you are to be distracted and "caught up" in BIG time wasters that are not propelling you toward your destiny.
- Finally, whenever possible, schedule your biggest tasks earlier in the morning or even before work hours. This habit will give you a head start and help you avoid the day-to-day distractions that happen during highly active business hours.

#4 NEGATIVE ADDICTIONS

Based on the statistics, science, and insights in the previous chapters, you should grasp how critically important it is that we practice caution every day regarding what we feed our minds and hearts.

All addictions carry the same characteristics. Whether it's the blings and dings of social media notifications or addictions to drugs, alcohol, pornography, gaming, sugar, etc., addictions all produce a chemical reaction that creates a false sense of comfort or pleasure. Because the chemical reactions are short-lived, these empty, destructive pleasures produce constant craving.

Addictions like gossip, criticizing, and bullying are no different. The thought processes produce the same "feel good" chemical reaction in us that produces dopamine, oxytocin, serotonin, and endorphins. When we listen to or participate in gossip, news programs, or discussions that focus on the downfalls or tragedies of others, in a crazy, sick way, this behavior makes us feel "good," — better, smarter, or more privileged.

We can also become addicted to negative attention, which sometimes happens after we suffer a tragedy or struggle. In the beginning, we appreciate the outpouring of love and attention, which is critical and life-giving during these times of life. If we're not careful, we can become dependent on these responses, which can lead us to subconsciously create negative mindsets that crave more of this type of attention, rather than striving to move beyond it.

In all cases of addiction, we must ask ourselves important questions and get honest about our answers:

- Are these behaviors benefiting me?
- Is focusing on these behaviors the best use of my time?
- What effects are they having on me? On others? On my family? On my future?
- Will continuing move me closer to my destiny or away from it?
- If I do not deal with this now, will I likely have regrets later in life?

SIX MORE GREAT FOCUS AND PRODUCTIVITY HACKS

#5 TAKE WALK BREAKS EVERY 60–90 MINUTES.

Stepping away from big projects every 60–90 minutes can recharge and refresh you. These breaks can trigger an onset of endorphins that will renew zeal, especially with projects that keep you seated too long. Even a 10–20-minute walk can increase brain activity, boost our immune system, and increase cognitive function.

#6 EVALUATE LENGTH OF MEETINGS.

One client approached me in frustration about being required to attend so many long meetings. She could not keep up with her projects or complete her deskwork. We discovered that most of the 1-hour meetings she attended only required her insights for 5–10 minutes, at most. She was given permission to appear for allocated time slots, which immediately resolved her issue. (Who in the world said we needed to have 1-hour meetings, anyway?)

#7 HOLD STANDING OR WALKING MEETINGS.

Both types of meetings keep attendees focused, interactive, and on point, not to mention, awake. Great thinkers like Steve Jobs, Harry Truman, Sigmund Freud, Aristotle, and Charles Dickens swore by standing or walking meetings. Benefits include better health, higher morale, and increased creativity, to name just a few.

#8 SCHEDULE 30-MINUTE "THINK TIMES."

We're often so wrapped up in doing things the way we've always done them that we miss out on discovering more efficient ways to do them. These tasks may be things we have done for years or even decades. Each week, schedule 10–30-minute "think times" to look at the items on your lists and then ask the following questions:

- Is there a more efficient way of doing this?
- Can I recruit, hire, or delegate this task and use my time more wisely?
- Is there a way I can do this task better if I gain the right education or ask for experienced advice?
- Is this something I really need to be giving my time and attention to?
- Can I creatively alter the process to make it faster, better, or more economical (i.e., think outside the box)?

#9 THE TWO-MINUTE RULE

If a task requires only two minutes to complete, don't put it off until later. We often bypass emails, procrastinate on small jobs, or neglect putting things in their place simply because we view the job as unimportant or boring. Procrastinating only adds to our burden and unnecessarily lengthens our task list. This reduces productivity, which causes more stress. Developing this one habit eliminates many of the "nagging" tasks we often delay completing.

#10 ACCOUNTABILITY

Seek out a mentor, coach, or accountability partner to share your vision with, to encourage your persistence, and to help you accomplish your goals. This goal is valuable and well worth any time or investment you might make to achieve. I often hear clients say that they know what to do but can't motivate themselves to do it. Verbalizing what we want to accomplish to another person can increase our commitment far beyond our ability to "go it alone." Great achievers always confess that they did not reach greatness alone.

> **REFRAME AND REWIRE TIP #9**
> Managing energy, focus, and time is more about managing YOU than it is about managing any obstacles you must overcome.

ROUTINE BUILDERS FROM CHAPTER NINE

Take a good look again at all ten tips offered in this chapter and assess the areas you need to work on. List them below, along with specific solutions you will carry out in order to improve in all three areas:

ENERGY

_____
_____
_____
_____
_____
_____

FOCUS

_____
_____
_____
_____
_____
_____

TIME

_____
_____
_____
_____
_____
_____

CHAPTER TEN

POWERFUL PRINCIPLES
OF INFLUENCE
AND GREATNESS

The number one need of all humans is so powerful that newborn infants have been known to physically perish when deprived of it. Despite age, background, gender, or position in life, everyone needs to feel what I call "Necessary Significance." From birth to death, we all pursue a place in society. We desire to be accepted, appreciated, valued, and recognized for our contributions to the world. We long to belong.

As children, we run to our parents and proudly show them our attempts at gymnastics, coloring, or art. Later in childhood and our teens, we try to impress our peers by showing off, in both good and bad ways. However, the goal is always the same: for others to recognize and appreciate what we can offer the world. Even as adults, we strive for better careers, higher positions, nicer houses, cars, or things that give us a sense of achievement. In the winter of our lives, we cherish the relationships of loved ones, ever longing for their presence near us. We hold tightly to fond memories and live for visits, phone calls, and cards or letters to remind us that we still matter. As I work with leaders and teams, I emphasize these facts because feeling significant is the most powerful principle in creating a culture where people thrive:

Teams develop strong loyalty when they know they are valued and what their expectations are. They want recognition for their gifts, talents, and experience. They also want opportunities to contribute to the success of their team. When people are appreciated and given a clear vision of their objectives, most teams go well beyond expectations.

This is also true in families, in communities, and in all people groups. **Necessary significance is the key to influence.** However, you cannot give to others what you do not possess yourself. If you struggle with unforgiveness (Chapter Six) or you have not worked on your heart and mind to develop powerful, confident, compassionate inner dialogue (Chapters One through Four) or if you have not developed the right heart energy (Chapter Five) you will not authentically practice the characteristics of influence.

12 CHARACTERISTICS OF INFLUENCE AND GREATNESS

The practices listed below are simply that: *practices*. You must work at them daily and expect them to take time to develop. As you work on YOU, other areas of your life will begin to fall into place. As stated before, there is no secret formula to success; you must be committed to consistent growth on this journey to reframe and rewire.

#1 — HUMILITY

Some would say humility means thinking less of yourself and more of others. This statement is quite general and can be translated two different ways:

The first and most common interpretation is that we rate ourselves below others and place ourselves last, which destroys our potential through negative inner dialogue, speech, and self-defeating habits. We may say things like:

- "I've always been sacrificial and put others before myself. It's just the way I am."
- "I just can't, you don't understand my schedule. Someday I intend to work on my growth and fitness, but right now, my family is more important."
- "You know me, a klutz and a procrastinator, lol! I've learned to live with it, and I'm fine."
- "It's just not my way of doing things. I'm a very nice person, but I've always been this way, and I don't intend to change for anyone."

These statements are deceptive because they make us feel better about ourselves, but they're actually a form of "false humility." They reflect a person who says that they're doing their best, but in their hearts they're looking for accolades or acceptance for their shortcomings.

The second way of interpreting this statement assumes the person makes effort and shows accountability. This form of humility is marked by truth, authenticity, compassion, and integrity.

People who exemplify true humility, which is less common, are never boastful. They think well of others but do not put themselves down in the process. They expect the best of themselves and never blame people or circumstances for things they are responsible for, such as their growth, their mistakes, and their shortcomings. They are not afraid to apologize when they hurt or offend someone, but they also don't "over-apologize."

True humility is demonstrated by a calm but strong state of mind that demonstrates that the person is fully aware and accountable for his/her behavior.

#2 — NOT EASILY OFFENDED

Imagine being invited to an elite event. You walk into a room filled with chandeliers and tables with white linen tablecloths, glistening silver, and china reflecting off the lights like diamonds in a clear stream. A sharply dressed man in a tuxedo seats you at a table filled with well-known and prestigious individuals who greet you. The purpose of the event is to recognize influencers who have significantly impacted society. Everyone at the table is enjoying the dinner portion of the event, including a performance. Energy and excitement laced with etiquette and courtesy fill the room. You are overwhelmed with a sense of privilege to be where you are.

The program begins with the emcee offering a brief introduction before the achievement award recipients are announced. One by one, the winners gracefully walk across the stage and humbly receive recognition.

About thirty minutes into the awards, you notice one of the members at your table becoming anxious. His face has become contorted in anger. Those at his table note his negative energy and restlessness. Several minutes later the last award is presented, and the room breaks into applause, followed by a standing ovation. However, the distressed man has become indignant and walks abruptly from the room, making it difficult for the remainder of the audience to rejoice in the excitement of the moment.

Soon after the man leaves, a woman approaches his table and inquires about his whereabouts. People at the table answer with uncertainty. She turns and walks toward the doors leading out of the room. Within moments, a loud voice is heard outside the back of the room, followed by shouting from other voices. The energy in the room has now shifted from a highly excited, positive experience to an unstable, anxious environment.

You look around and notice audience members with mixed emotions. Some people are chatting amongst themselves with concern, while others remain focused on celebrating the winners' accomplishments.

The emcee clears his throat, and the crowd slowly settles down. There is now one empty chair at your table, and it has become evident that the man who once sat there became offended in some way and is not returning.

You just witnessed how one person's offense can affect an entire group of people—in this example, people who gathered to celebrate influencers and recognize kindness in a hurting world.

Note the distinct shift of energy that took place in the room and think about when you've witnessed a similar scene.

For instance, at the airport when a traveler harshly disputes a disagreement with the ticket counter agent, affecting everyone around them, including staff, those in line, and other people who are observing.

How about the time your spouse offended you with a remark—a remark you chose to stew on for an entire day, affecting your attitude at work, prodding you to act curtly and impatiently with co-workers? Then you returned home still carrying that vile and negative mindset and infected everyone in your household.

The things of value we accomplish in our lives are robbed of their value when we allow offenses to seep into our attitude and eradicate the positive things we've worked to accomplish.

Think for a moment about offensive events that have occurred in your life, whether you were offended or the offender. How did the attitude you chose influence others and affect them for good or for evil?

Offending others isn't a goal for most people, even when the offense may be justified. But offenses are common, and we have to deal with them every day. We often carry offenses from long-past events. Other offending wounds may be fresh in our minds. If you desire to be influential and possess "magnetism," you must determine that when offenses come, you will choose to react in a way that makes others stand amazed at your resilience and emotional intelligence. This doesn't mean we won't need time to process hurts or occasionally scream into a pillow. It just means that influential people don't allow offenses to consume and control them.

Ask yourself this question: "Do I know anyone who is constantly offended, yet well-thought-of and highly successful?" Chances are, your answer is *no*.

> *"The problem is not the problem;*
> *the problem is your attitude about the problem."*
> —Captain Jack Sparrow, *Pirates of the Caribbean*

#3 — EMPOWERING AND THOUGHTFUL
A quote that I shared previously in this book bears repeating:

> *"People don't care how much you know*
> *until they know how much you care."*
> – Theodore Roosevelt

We build our future based upon how we perceive ourselves. Yes, how we perceive ourselves reflects how others see us. If your inner dialogue focuses on how you can promote yourself and help others recognize your significance, you create the reverse of what you desire. Some people will see you as selfish and lacking confidence, while others will see you as a "victim," always looking for someone to feel sorry for you or give you a "break." You will struggle trying to establish relationships because, subconsciously, you make people feel unimportant because you focus on YOU, rather than others.

This perplexing situation often becomes a vicious cycle. People frequently become unknowingly caught in this trap. They desperately want to be liked, valued, and acknowledged; however, because they listen to negative inner dialogue, they constantly struggle with how they feel about themselves and how others perceive them. This only makes them try harder to be recognized, like a teenager who constantly acts out. The teenager doesn't wake up each day thinking about how he or she can get into trouble; rather, they think about what they can do to be regarded as important and to be noticed by their peers.

If you want to be influential, make it a goal each day to *be thoughtful* and *look for opportunities to empower others*. Below are a few tips:

- Remember people's names and use them when you're talking to them.
- Recognize the accomplishments and/or feelings of others.
- Pay attention to them and do things to make them feel valued and significant.
- Ask them questions.
- Look for opportunities to praise.
- Listen without interrupting or forcing your agenda.

> *"Successful people are always looking for opportunities to help others. Unsuccessful people are always asking, "What's in it for me?"*
>
> — Brian Tracy

#4 — CHEERFUL

Earlier in my career, I had the opportunity to build and lead teams. Every six months, I'd conduct a team satisfaction survey. This gave me the opportunity to learn how I was doing and what kind of culture I was developing. I remember one specific time when one of my support managers wrote, "You're a very knowledgeable and compassionate leader. However, you could smile more. People on the team who don't know you as I do often misconstrue your demeanor simply because you don't smile enough." This observation stuck with me, and I made a genuine effort to smile more.

I'm not saying that leaders or anyone must smile all the time. However, when we do smile, we become approachable, and we change the energy around us. I can think of several instances when a simple smile altered the environment and the mood of those in it. Furthermore, smiling is infectious, and when we smile, we encourage others to reciprocate.

It's also important to note that smiling releases dopamine, endorphins, and serotonin into our body chemistry, and these chemicals create a sense of happiness and can instantly lift our mood.

#5 — SOCIALLY INTELLIGENT

It goes without saying that we must be socially intelligent to be influential. Obviously, we cannot expect to influence others if we struggle to get along with them.

Socially intelligent people show genuine interest in others. They come across as sincere and thoughtful. Socially intelligent people leave others feeling positive about themselves, about others, and about the world in general.

One who is socially intelligent tends to be genuinely concerned about the affairs, thoughts, feelings, and challenges of other people.

They are not interested from a standpoint of intrusion, judgment, or pity, but from a perspective of interest and helping others "rethink" their perceptions. This is done through encouragement, kind words, listening, believing in people, and never forcing their ideas on someone else.

For example, a leader who is socially intelligent will not simply provide answers when things go wrong. Instead, they raise the potential of their team by drawing out *their* creative solutions and empowering them to overcome adversity, while reassuring them that their leader believes in them.

> *"Leadership is not about titles, positions or flowcharts.*
> *It is about one life influencing another."*
> — John C. Maxwell

Another example of social intelligence can be seen in business transactions. This means that when we work with potential clients, we listen in order to understand and remain open to new ways of strategizing. We clearly and effectively reflect back client concerns, assuring them that we can see the issues from their perception. Our suggested solutions will align with our client's needs because we take the time to listen, learn, and adapt to the client or the organization's core issues.

In summary, social intelligence requires approaching all conversations and challenges with the intent of leaving people better off than we found them.

> *"Most people do not listen with the intent to*
> *understand; they listen with the intent to reply."*
> — Stephen R. Covey

#6 — ENCOURAGING

In the beginning of this chapter, I mentioned "Necessary Significance," a vital need we all share, no matter our title, position, or experiences in life. Encouraging others is one of the simplest forms of providing significance to others. We can completely alter how someone sees themselves and their future when we take time to tell someone, "Great job!" or "I am proud of you!" or "I know you can do this; I believe in you!"

Encouragement is not about flattery. It is about authentically recognizing the abilities, talents, and contributions of others. True encouragement can vastly improve people's perceptions of themselves and empower them to step into areas where they would otherwise struggle to succeed. Encouragement can also be used to reinforce behaviors we want repeated.

Consider the following relationships and visualize potential outcomes if/when you consistently applied encouragement.

- Spouse or significant other
- Your children or other children in your life
- Family members/relatives (especially those you may not currently get along with)
- Your supervisor or leader
- Your friends
- Co-workers
- Colleagues
- Strangers you meet every day

When you create a habit of encouraging others, you become unforgettable. When people think of who is valuable to them, who to invite to special occasions, who to consider for job offers or great opportunities, they will think of you because you encourage them and boost their confidence.

#7 — ACCEPTING AND EMPATHETIC

Showing empathy toward others and respecting their differences is one of the most powerful ways to create life influence.

When we are offended, we often push people away and create poor relational experiences. We experience the same results when we judge others or do not accept them for who they're created to be. We're often tempted to judge or criticize people when we don't understand their perceptions because they see things differently than we do. We jump to conclusions and assumptions, thinking we know what's best for others.

I heard about an incident that recently occurred at an airport. A group of people assembled at the bottom of an escalator, awaiting a tramcar to transport them to their flight gate. An older couple stood amongst them, trying to speak to one another above the noise of the crowd. Out of the corner of their eyes, the couple noticed a very large woman coming down the escalator. Without realizing how loud his voice was, the old man turned to his wife and said, "Look at her; that's just awful! Why doesn't she do something about her weight?"

Most likely, the heavyset woman already felt uncomfortable about being in public, and she must have known other people would stare and talk about her. The man at the bottom of the escalator had spoken in a tone loud enough to carry, so people heard him and turned to look in the large woman's direction. Within seconds, the woman noticed the crowd at the bottom of the escalator staring at her. She was now close enough to hear what they were saying about her. As she passed through the crowd, everyone could see that her eyes were red and welling up with tears. We can assume that the old man meant no harm by his words, yet the woman certainly felt harm.

Do we know what the woman on the escalator had experienced in her life? Can we rightfully judge why she was the size she was? Do we know and have compassion for the story behind her obesity?

And furthermore, what was so important that she was forced to muster the courage to travel that day, knowing she would be publicly judged and condemned for her weight? On a day when she needed acceptance and empathy the most, she received judgment and condemnation.

How often are we guilty of this same thought process? How often do we judge, condemn, assume, and criticize others? And more importantly, how does our condemning attitude influence us, those judged, and the people and culture around us? Do our attitudes make the world a better place? Do they move us toward greatness, leadership, and positions of influence? Or are we appropriately shamed by our answers to these questions?

How about road rage? Do you become inflamed when others cut you off in traffic but expect kindness when *you* cut someone off? Have you ever made an assumption or a statement about someone that you had to apologize for later, and then when the same thing was done to you, you held a grudge against your offender?

Accepting others' differences without judgment is a trademark of an influential person. People feel safe when they trust that their feelings, ideas, or concerns will be respected and valued.

When people don't hear you judge and criticize others, they feel confident that you are a person of integrity and honor. This, in turn, creates rare, powerful admiration and respect. Showing empathy and respecting differences are two of the most powerful ways to build influence in your life.

#8 — GRATITUDE

In Chapter Five, we covered the power of heart energy and emotions, which can be measured in magnetometers. Gratitude measures as one of the most powerful emotions, emitting 500–600 magnetometers. In fact, it is psychologically impossible to feel a deep sense of gratitude and complain or be vindictive at the same time.

Gratitude has the power to heal the mind and heart of past hurts and tragedies. Those who choose to think about what they are grateful for every day will feel stronger, healthier, and more well-adjusted.

Some people might react by saying, "Well, if you knew my life and what's happened to me, you'd agree that I have nothing to be grateful about."

When we choose to believe this, we're lying to ourselves or looking for excuses to stay bitter. We can be grateful for breath, strength, trees, flowers, the sun, the moon, loved ones, faith, values, beliefs, etc. We have so many things to be grateful for that I could not list them all, even if I wrote many more chapters.

One of the assignments I give clients as part of their "brain training" is to list nine things each week to be grateful for, and then think about them each day. This "Attitude of Gratitude" becomes a habit and alters your physiology (Chapters Three and Four). The more you do to maintain a sense of gratitude, the more you will bring about a change in your perspective that will become evident to everyone around you. Everyone wants to be around someone who is consistently grateful, just as people want to stay away from those who are consistently ungrateful.

I'd like to challenge you at this point:

Create a "gratitude list" and post it where you will see it (i.e., bathroom mirror or dressing area). Then, every day first thing in the morning, and again before going to bed, speak the items on your list aloud with genuine feelings of gratitude. Do this for one full week. If you're diligent, you'll begin to notice a difference in the way you feel, both intrinsically and extrinsically.

#9 — AUTHENTICITY AND TRANSPARENCY

It's in our nature to hide our flaws and shortcomings for fear that others might think less of us. Because of this, we wear masks in a defensive attempt to "protect" the real us and keep people from seeing who we "really are."

Living this way creates unnecessary stress because we're forced to work very hard to stay "undercover." Masking our true selves only increases our insecurities, making life even more difficult. Living this kind of façade is exhausting and phony.

Challenge yourself in the area of authenticity. The truth is, we have more trust and appreciation for people who authentically own up to their shortcomings, gracefully accept their flaws, and even laugh at themselves. People more readily identify with others who acknowledge that they're less than perfect than they do with people who pretend to be perfect.

Giving yourself *permission to be you* sets you free! It also opens up possibilities to express yourself, which can lead to better relationships, new job offers, and other amazing opportunities.

Make it your goal to be the best version of you every day. Ignore the critics and stop trying to be someone else. Just BE REAL!

> *"Have fun, be crazy, be weird. Go out and screw up! You're going to anyway, so you might as well enjoy the process."*
> — Tony Robbins

#10 — GENEROSITY

All of us have a desire to give back to something bigger than ourselves, to make an impact, and to create a difference for others in our sphere of influence. However, those who are influential also develop the habit of looking for opportunities to give back.

When we build a reputation for generosity, people take notice. Whether it's giving to causes for children, veterans, physical disabilities, or diseases, the rapport we gain is undefinable in terms of cost or investment.

Some people reason that they would give if they had the money to do so. However, being generous is not confined to monetary giving. Below is a list of other ways you can develop a reputation as a generous person.

- Volunteer for a soup kitchen or other homeless cause.
- Share insights freely through speaking pro bono at events, sitting on panels, or in one-on-one conversation.
- Offer your expertise on a board.
- Run or bike in a marathon to raise money for a cause.
- Hold an event and promise a percentage of proceeds to a chosen cause.
- Buy meals, toys, or gifts for the less fortunate during the holidays.
- Donate or help put together care packets for a cause.

This list could go on and on, but this gives you a few ideas to begin with. Giving of your time, insights, expertise, or resources is never wasted and is a cornerstone characteristic of someone who is influential. **The world needs more generous people; make sure you are one of them.**

#11 — INTEGRITY

Integrity is high on a priority list of needed character qualities. Even if you represent all ten qualities listed thus far, if you do not have integrity, you are immediately disqualified as a person of influence.

According to businessdictionary.com, the definition of *integrity* is "the quality of being honest and having strong moral principles; moral uprightness."

Without integrity, you become untrustworthy, appear unstable, and ultimately damage your rapport. Even if you lose trust in only one transaction or relationship, your integrity becomes compromised.

Years ago, I assisted in hiring a manager for a team I was building. The individual seemed authentic in the interview. They had a college degree, great experience, and their references checked out positively. For months, they performed every task with precision and excellence. This person also connected well with the team. However, they began asking a lot of questions about the history of the organization, certain individuals, and leadership.

At first, their questions seemed innocent and inquisitive. Then they started going out of their way to create a relationship with the executive leadership team, more specifically, the leader responsible for *their* supervisor. Over time, this employee collected and used information they had collected to manipulate their way into the supervisor's position and get them fired.

They held on to the new position for about six months, but eventually, the web they'd spun began to unravel, revealing many lies, including lies they'd told in the initial pre-hire interview. Their integrity was immediately compromised. They were terminated, leaving a very poor reputation behind, along with a badly shaken team that needed extra care in order to regain trust and momentum, to rebuild.

Going back to the story I told near the beginning of this chapter about offense, one person can create a great deal of damage in a brief amount of time—for themselves and those around them. The difference between the story of offense and this story is that you can often redeem the damage caused by offense with an apology and a change in behavior.

With integrity, however, reconciliation is not that simple. Once you have created an untrustworthy, selfish reputation, turning it around can take many months or even years. In some cases, if the damage is too great, integrity can never be restored in the hearts of those who have been affected most.

> *"When you are able to maintain your own highest standard of integrity—regardless of what others may do— you are destined for greatness."*
> —Napoleon Hill

#12 — CONFIDENCE

Confidence is the core of greatness. Confidence is being willing to take risks; it is standing firm on what you believe in; it is not being afraid to become the person you were created to be. Confidence gives us the courage to step out beyond ourselves to pursue our dreams. Confidence empowers us to live in the moment and remain authentic in who we truly are. Confidence is dancing in the rain or singing in the middle of a crowd. When someone is confident— clear about their core values and comfortable in their own skin—we desire to follow them.

It is a deception to believe that some are born with confidence and others are not. **All of us possess the ability and obligation to become confident in who we are.** All of us should make it a priority to daily work on improving our confidence.

What is the Process?

As stated throughout this book, the process of gaining confidence is experienced as we consistently implement our daily routine. From the moment we open our eyes to the instant we close them at night, our confidence grows in our thoughts, our hearts, and is seared upon our subconscious each day as we continue our journey to reframe and rewire. A few questions to ask yourself:

- What is my inner dialogue upon waking in the morning?
- How do I speak to and about myself, internally and externally, throughout the day?
- Do I offer myself the same grace and empathy that I do when others fail or make mistakes?
- Am I willing to step out of my "comfort zone" to meet new faces, take risks, and be who I am created to be?
- Do I spend time each day increasing my gifts, talents, and knowledge to better myself?

We should ask ourselves these questions and others every day. If we fail to do so, we create a chasm in our "inner person," an emptiness, a feeling of unworthiness, which is the root of poor confidence.

#13 — VISIONARY

It is not enough to share a vision with a colleague, an organization, or even a community. You must have a vision for yourself. **Vision is the tie that binds the accomplishments of today to the possibilities of tomorrow. Vision is the hub of your universe, the compass of your journey, and the climax of your destiny, all at once.**

A visionary lights the way and attracts others to walk with them into the light. They rejoice in hope and excitement the moment the sun hits their face in the morning. People with vision walk taller and appear more resolved because they're assured of their purpose and where they're headed with each step. Their purpose empowers them with strength and tenacity to accomplish things that others would deem impossible. In the Western world, people like Martin Luther King Jr., Steve Jobs, Arnold Schwarzenegger, Oprah Winfrey, Eleanor Roosevelt, Thomas Edison, the Wright brothers, and many more tenacious individuals blazed trails as visionaries. They possessed an unstoppable mindset and pursued their dreams against all odds. Despite failures, criticism, lack of funding, credentials, shortcomings, and hardships, they endured.

Whether you admire these individuals is of no consequence. No one can refute that they each pursued a vision that materialized from nothing. In fact, many of them started with no money and no influence, only the power of the indomitable human spirit.

"Where there is no vision, the people perish."
—Proverbs 29:18

All of the Characteristics of Greatness and Influence carry distinct importance in your pursuit for greatness. As you determine what decisions to make in the road ahead, keep in mind that, ultimately, we do not become what others say we are; we become who *we* say we are. If you hope to reach the fullness of your potential, you must invest in YOU!

REFRAME AND REWIRE TIP #11
There are two kinds of people in the world:

1. Those who are interested and have good intentions.
2. Those who are committed, at any cost.

Are you INTERESTED or COMMITTED?

TENTH ASSIGNMENT

Number a paper from 1–13 or write below. Then take time to look at the 13 Characteristics and honestly assess where you are in each by rating yourself on a scale of 1–10. A rating of one means you are really struggling, and ten means you have formed solid habits and live out that characteristic consistently. Develop a plan for growth for any areas where you rated yourself five or less.

1. _____	
2. _____	
3. _____	
4. _____	
5. _____	
6. _____	
7. _____	
8. _____	
9. _____	
10. _____	
11. _____	
12. _____	
13. _____	

11 TIPS AND TOOLS TO BUILD YOUR SUCCESS ROUTINE

The purpose of this book is to help you understand that what you do every day of your life determines your destiny, personally and professionally. I would like to use these last two chapters to provide tangible "helps." They will equip you to reframe and rewire so you can overcome persistent behaviors and habits that pull you away from your destiny, rather than push you toward it. As you read these tips, use the section at the end of this chapter to formulate your new daily routine.

11 TIPS AND TOOLS:

1. GRATITUDE LIST

Write and rewrite a weekly gratitude list to post and read daily. Make this a lifelong habit and be certain to express true inner gratitude when referring to it. Psychologically, you cannot be frustrated and grateful at the same time. This tool will empower you to maintain high heart energy and keep you focused on building the right neural pathways. Consider reading the list every morning as soon as you wake up.

2. NOTE CARDS

Maintaining the right thoughts and responding in excellent ways throughout the day can be challenging. Purchase a stack of index cards to write out reminders, quotes, tips, victories, or encouraging words to remind you as often as you need reminding. Brain training takes effort, and each rogue thought must be "reined in" immediately, in order to prevent the regrowth of bad neural networks while you are promoting good ones.

Carry the cards like tools in your toolbox. Post them everywhere and anywhere you find helpful: bathroom mirror, computer, car dashboard, refrigerator, wallet or purse, etc. In the beginning, these cards may be the "lifeline" you need to support new ways of thinking, but in time, you won't need them as often.

3. JOURNALING

For centuries, journaling has been used as an outstanding method of therapy that surpasses many other methods. It is a private place of neurological expression that helps us effectively process and "dump" frustrations, concerns, ideas, thoughts, or events. In fact, writing is a form of cognitive restructuring. When we write, we reflect and reframe the words we have written, which helps give us a new outlook. Journaling can also be a place where new ideas spring forth and inspire us, while providing a place to record ideas for later use.

Finally, a journal is a fantastic way to observe our growth and progress. Take time—weekly, monthly, or quarterly—to page back through and observe how many changes you've made as you read. For example, things that once upset you no longer do. New ideas have come to fruition. Prayers or thoughts you projected onto the pages have materialized, giving you new hope and zeal for what is possible.

4. MASTER LIST AND TASK LISTS

Nothing can inspire you more than a feeling of accomplishment and progress! Each year create a "Master List" of everything you want to accomplish, both personally and professionally. Then prioritize the items and keep the list where you can refer to it frequently. Each week or month, select one to three items and schedule time to work on them. For more details on using this list effectively, refer to Chapter Nine on Focus and Productivity Hacks. Download the Master List template at *reframeandrewire.com*.

5. SPECIAL DAYS

All of us lead busy lives, so finding time to spend with family or friends can be challenging. If we're not intentional about setting aside time for relationships, moments will keep slipping away. Eventually, we'll realize we haven't given needed time to those we care about. This can cause unintended and unnecessary stress in our relationships. Adopting a habit of "Special Days" can help alleviate this problem.

For a significant other, choose one evening of the week for a "Date Night." Although this may seem difficult, remember that greatness comes from the investments we make each day in ourselves and in our vital relationships. Keep it simple and live in the moment, but commit to a date night. Treat this time as you would an important client appointment or a meeting with an admired colleague.

However, don't stop there. Appoint a special day to each of your children, your parents, and any other relationships you value. On that day or evening, devote *all* of your attention to that person, with no interruptions and no cell phone. Play cards/games, go for walks, create projects, or do anything you both enjoy. As each week comes and goes, those who are dear to you will see that you value them and want to spend time with them. Your relationships will benefit as you sow critical seeds of time and attention.

You will also shed former guilt you may have carried. On busy or bad days, remind yourself and your loved ones that their day is coming, and you're truly looking forward to your time with them. Consistency will require forethought, planning, and even sacrifice, but you will never regret investing your time in valued relationships.

6. VISIONEERING TOOLS

Since we already covered the power of visualizing, there is no need to go back over it. Many of you may have heard of a "vision board." If you haven't, I encourage you to seek out images of vision boards on the internet so you can see what they look like. I suggest several alternate tools that are much easier to create and just as effective.

Vision Paper

Vision boards can seem daunting and burdensome. Because of this, they often end up an unfinished project. Even if they are completed, finding a good spot to place them where they don't lose their impact is another challenge. Sometimes it's best to simplify.

Start with a blank Word document or an 8.5 x 11 sheet of paper and place six images that are significant to you on it. Add comments or quotes under each one to describe what is in your heart about that image. If you have a computer, search for images there. If you don't, you can draw pictures or paste cutouts from a magazine. The project should take no more than 5–15 minutes to complete. You can duplicate or post these papers in multiple places, then change them as each picture (goal) comes to fruition.

---

* Theta is a brain wave pattern that is between asleep and awake.

Vision Cards

If you did the exercise in Chapter Two, you should have a well-written *Personal Vision Statement*. Write it on the "Note Cards" listed above until you memorize it. You can also obtain business card stock and write or print your vision statement on cards that you can take with you everywhere.

7. TRIGGERS

It can feel overwhelming to try to remember so many new things when you're setting up a new routine. Our tendency is to fall back into old habits. However, we must change the familiar. For instance, if we want to exercise and read more, perhaps we should break the habit of looking in the refrigerator or turning on the television when we arrive home each day. Triggers are a great way to help you create desired new habits. The best way to create effective triggers is to apply Henry Ford's adage: "If you always do what you've always done, you will always get what you have always got." Therefore, you must develop triggers that are different from your norm. Below are examples mentioned earlier and ideas for each:

> **Exercise Daily**—choose the same time of day to adopt this habit. Then attach the thought of exercising to another habit or event that occurs at that same time each day. For instance, if you choose to take a walk after work every day, you might attach the activity to removing your work shoes or walking through the entry of your home. If you have a pet, when you see your pet when you arrive home, remind yourself to go for a walk. In time, taking a walk will become an unconscious habit.

Read Daily—You can apply the same trigger as described above for exercise, or you can set an alarm. You could make reading into an enjoyable event to help you prepare for the day, unwind, or go to sleep at night. Curl up with your favorite beverage in your favorite chair and make reading something you look forward to.

Stop Looking in the Refrigerator—I had a client who stopped this and lost over fifteen pounds. She simply wrote herself a kind note and placed it on the refrigerator door as a reminder to drink water or go for a walk instead.

Here is an example:

"Dear _____, Welcome home! Grab a glass of water and go for a walk—you will thank me later!"

Triggers can be set up in a multitude of ways to create new habits. In time, the notes, alarms, and choice points will no longer be necessary. You will be on autopilot, doing these things automatically, just like you do with showering and brushing your teeth.

8. DAILY INSPIRATION

Once you finish this book, you might feel excited about creating your success routine, and you may do an excellent job putting one together. However, as with all new things, we can lose our initial fervor. The idea is to stay inspired and motivated every day. I accomplish this and help clients accomplish this through daily morning inspiration. I've developed the habit of listening to something inspiring, educational, or motivational as soon as I get up in the morning—preferably, something related to my vision for the future. My selection could be an audio book, an online source, or something pre-recorded. This way, I keep my thoughts intentional while my brain waves are still coming out of theta* and are open to suggestion. I keep the audio running throughout my morning routine: exercising, showering, making breakfast for the family, primping for the day, etc. On a typical day, by the time I finish my power hour and morning preparations, I will have listened to anywhere from an hour and a half to two hours of inspiring messages. I even prefer to listen to something intentional in the car, rather than the radio, during my commute time.

The BONUS to listening during my morning routine is that my family hears these messages, too. They benefit greatly, even on days when they're not giving their full attention. Imagine listening to intentional, inspiring messages instead of dreaded "news" or other distractions. Seeking inspiration by listening during a morning routine or other structured time can change the atmosphere of your home and, undoubtedly, the atmosphere of your heart and mind. If you remember Jen's story in Chapter One, this practice healed her marriage.

The second way to attain daily inspiration is by reading books or articles. Choose materials that will increase your resolve for success and equip you to meet the challenges you face with needed confidence.

I attribute the habit of daily inspiration to be one of the most important aspects of reframing and rewiring.

9. TECHNOLOGY

For those of you who own devices such as cellular phones, tablets, computers, and the like, there is really no excuse for not using these devices to empower, equip, and engage you in reframing and rewiring. You can download apps for exercise, meditation, scheduling, journaling, as well as alarms and reminders, and inspirational websites for daily growth. Devices can be a distraction or a gift. It all depends on how you choose to use them.

For readers who do not possess or desire to possess technology, think about creative ways that you can use the "silent moments of the day" to alter your state of mind. Try singing, speaking positive affirmations over yourself, reading, meditating, or listening to the sounds of nature.

10. AFFIRMATIONS

In Chapter Three, we discussed forms of cognitive restructuring, and I provided a list of affirmations for you. This tool is a key piece for setting up a daily routine that brings about transformation. However, if affirmations are not done properly, they are "pointless repetitions." I implement affirmations in the morning while I'm on my recumbent bicycle. Some of my clients place them on their bathroom mirrors. Other clients like to speak their affirmations while they're in the car driving. I am not advocating reading while driving, only pointing out that a physical list isn't needed for affirmations.

Whatever your method of implementing affirmations, speak them applying authentic emotion, visualization, and focus. This is the only way to produce the connection needed for real change. Unless you engage your heart, mind, and soul, affirmations do not produce the necessary electromagnetic energy to build new neural networks, alter physiology, release neurotransmitters, and change your heart energy. Without the critical component of sincerity, speaking affirmations is like turning on a lamp that's not plugged in; sincerity is the power or the current that lights up the lamp.

11. RELEASE ENDORPHINS

In response to physical exercise, the pituitary gland floods the body with endorphins, and they can remain in the bloodstream for up to 48 hours providing a multitude of benefits, including:

- Reduced cortisol, the stress hormone
- Better sleep cycles
- Heightened immune system
- Prevention of anxiety and depression
- Reduced pain and inflammation
- Increased pleasure centers, producing more serotonin and dopamine

Endorphins play a role in creating the feeling of euphoria often experienced by runners, known as "runner's high" that can provide a powerful dose of pain relief.

As you build your new daily routine, do not leave out physical activity. Plan to exercise a minimum of 20–30 minutes per day, at least 3–5 days per week. If you can do more than this, the benefits will increase. **Daily, consistent activity is an infusion of power like no other.**

Try some of these methods of exercise:

- Recumbent bicycling or bicycling
- Walking or running
- Treadmill walking (I do this an average of 5 miles per day at my desk while working)
- Yoga
- Aerobics
- Various dance or kickboxing classes
- Working out at the gym
- Lifting weights

The list is endless, but you must discover a routine that works for you. You **must** create space for exercise. If you try to squeeze it in when it seems convenient or when you feel like it, you will never become consistent, and you will never experience its benefits. You might feel like you tried, and it didn't work for you; however, only those who create a dedicated, consistent program of daily exercise reap the benefits.

Consider exercising with a partner or making exercise a family activity. If that isn't possible, think about how you can make it fun or productive. I typically speak my affirmations while riding my recumbent bicycle or listening to inspirational or educational material with my earbuds during my floor exercises. Whatever *you* choose to do must become a ritual or daily habit. I chose to wake up early in the morning, which works fantastic for me (see Chapter Two for my morning daily routine).

This list is just a start. Many more tools are available. I sincerely hope these suggestions and resources will help you to get a solid start on what it takes to create and maintain a new lifestyle of achievement, opportunity, growth, and destiny-defining direction. Reframing and rewiring is for those who want to leave their comfort zone and stop coasting through life. And the good news is that anyone from any stage of life or status in life can build a new daily routine.

Below is a module you can use to create your new daily routine. You can also find this module online at *reframeandrewire.com*.

REFRAME AND REWIRE TIP #11
Any project that takes effort and focus will come together more efficiently with the right tools. The same is true with a success routine. When proper tools are in place and consistently used, the odds of achievement are greatly increased.

ELEVENTH ASSIGNMENT
BUILDING MY DAILY ROUTINE FOR GREATNESS

My Vision Statement is:

My Specific Goals for working toward daily growth are:

1. _____
2. _____
3. _____
4. _____
5. _____

I will awake each day at:

Immediately upon awakening, I will:

1. _____
2. _____
3. _____
4. _____
5. _____

While driving, I will listen to:

1. _____
2. _____
3. _____
4. _____
5. _____

I will learn to control my thoughts and attitudes throughout the day by using these tools:

1. _____
2. _____
3. _____
4. _____
5. _____

Upon arriving home, I will immediately:

1. _____
2. _____
3. _____
4. _____
5. _____

I will spend my evenings on vision-aligned activities of value, such as:

1. _____
2. _____
3. _____
4. _____
5. _____

Before retiring to bed, I will prime my subconscious toward right thinking in the following ways:

1. _____
2. _____
3. _____
4. _____
5. _____

I commit to work on the following additional habits:

1. _____
2. _____
3. _____
4. _____
5. _____

CHAPTER TWELVE

APPLYING YOUR NEW ROUTINE AND ACTING UPON YOUR VISION

"Life does not happen TO us; life happens FOR us."

–JIM CARREY

NTENTIONALITY is the best word to describe the purpose of this book. There are two groups of people in this world:

GROUP #1

Those who live life as it comes, going day-to-day expending their energy and thoughts on past and present problems. They typically "settle" with whatever hand life deals them. This group frequently becomes entrenched in debating what is wrong with the world. It seems the only way they can rise above problems is to pull others down.

This group traps themselves in a limited vision of life beneath the weight of reactive thoughts and actions. They live each day dulled by the same routine, unchallenged by the same perceptions, content with the same level of knowledge, embracing the same standards, yet expecting different results. When nothing improves, they grumble, find fault, or degrade themselves for their "limitations." They refuse to explore or examine why their ship doesn't come in and their life circles in a monotonous loop.

Living with this group's mindset produces a victim's mentality. Victims are often broken, discouraged, and feel as if the odds are stacked against them. They typically embrace a survival mentality of "just getting by," denying there are other choices and possibilities while criticizing those who find a better way. They often judge and mock those who are willing to step up to make their dreams happen, because victims are not willing to do what it takes to change.

GROUP #2

This group refuses to accept the "status quo." They're unwilling to watch life "happen" to them. The individuals who make up this group represent about 10 percent of the entire population, according to most statistics.[30]

Each day, they awake with zeal and energy for the opportunity of another day to work purposefully to see their dreams come to fruition. They often arise in the early hours of the morning, long before sunrise, spending the first hours of the day empowering themselves by creating strong minds and bodies.

Typically, this group has just as many problems as the first group but is unwilling to allow their problems to overtake them. Instead, they choose to use their problems as opportunities for growth, becoming better, instead of bitter about life.

They have clear vision, purpose, and create plans to carry out their vision, no matter what it takes. This group is relentless and takes 100 percent responsibility for where they are today and where they will be tomorrow. Whenever they encounter setbacks, critics, tragedies, or failures, they bounce back quickly and search for answers, spending little or no time on negative influences or mindsets.

The members of Group 2 spend each day with intentionality, making the most of every moment and investing their time in things that push them toward their destiny. They know their priorities and limit their commitments to things that are important to them. This group is one of the most misunderstood groups in society.

Some people think of the members of Group 2 as weird, zealous, over passionate, irritatingly positive, or (my personal favorite) "just lucky." The truth is that the majority of these people started with few or no advantages.

Which group do you wish to identify with? You are never too old or too young to make that choice, and it is **your** choice to make.

Below is a brief list of people who started with absolutely nothing and faced seemingly insurmountable odds. Yet, they all rose to the top, despite minimal or no support:

- Jim Carrey, Actor/Comedian
- Dr. Seuss, Children's Book Writer
- Claude Monet, Artist
- Thomas Edison, Inventor
- Michael Jordan, Athlete
- Steven Spielberg, Writer/Director
- Les Brown, Motivational Speaker
- Sam Walton, Retailer
- The Beatles, Musicians
- Vincent VanGogh, Painter
- Charles Schultz, Cartoonist
- Elvis Presley, King of Rock and Roll
- Demi Moore, Actress
- Kevin Plank, Clothing Creator/Founder

- Soichiro Honda, Engineer/Founder
- Oprah Winfrey, Journalist/TV Talk Show Host/Actress/CEO
- Steven King, Author of Thrillers
- Steve Harvey, Comedian/Speaker
- Leonardo DiCaprio, Actor
- Emily Dickenson, Poet
- Thomas Jefferson, President
- John Paul DeJoria, Entrepreneur/Hair Care
- Billy Graham, World Renowned Evangelist

If you desire more inspiration, I encourage you to look up these individuals' stories. You will quickly realize how these ordinary people, just like you and me, chose not to "settle." Against all odds, they tapped into their God-given talents, resolved to be intentional, worked hard, and found their way.

DAILY CHOOSING TO REFRAME AND REWIRE TO ACHIEVE GREATNESS THROUGH ROUTINE

If you have read and applied all that is in this book, you are now equipped to reframe and rewire for a new way of living that has the power to transform your future both personally and professionally. As long as you continue to apply your routine daily, the sky is the limit!

The benefits of reframing and rewiring are endless. I've listed just a few:

- Stronger and healthier relationships, i.e., family, spouse, friends, etc.
- Greater resilience in times of tragedy or trial
- A powerful force in your career, increasing your influence, and setting you up for promotion
- A stronger state of mind and greater peace in your life
- New open doors of opportunity, personally and professionally

- More energy, better physical health, and clearer daily vision
- Greater confidence and a relentless mindset
- The potential springboard to unexpected professional endeavors, such as a new business or career

I've had multiple clients start and succeed in new business endeavors! Most of them did not intend to begin a new business venture before they began our coaching relationship. One example is a client who inherited an estate with acreage that was in a perfect location to house a company. My client had a love for and experience with a business they wanted to start, but for various reasons an offer to obtain needed property had fallen through. However, they did not give up. The spark was lit, and their new daily routine was the fuel that set them ablaze to find another way.

Long story short, they learned how to start the business they desired from home and followed through with licensing to sell their own products. They now have their own brand, along with multiple buyers and plans to go into business full-time. Their family is elated at the idea! Consistently empowering their minds and hearts opened doors to a new world outside of their "normal" day-to-day. Since the time that I wrote this book, this client has maintained their new daily routine. They continue to see dreams come to fruition through the power of reframing and rewiring.

Contrariwise, one of my clients progressed very quickly through our coaching relationship and was extremely excited to build their new routine. Not far into their coaching, they birthed a concept for a business that had the potential to transform their life. It was a much-needed idea, unique to their industry. They studied and worked hard to create their first prototype, which got better and better with each revision. For a novice in their area of business, they produced results that were nothing short of amazing!

I was sure they would take their business to the next level. However, soon after our coaching relationship ended, they allowed negativity to creep back into their mindset, and they stopped their new daily routine. Within weeks, they slipped back into their old routines, and their dreams quickly faded, along with their state of mind.

The lesson here is that whatever you gain from this book, from other books, or from a coach, if you do not **build and maintain** new, lasting habits, you will end up right back where you started. Unfortunately for this second client, the probability is that the new neural networks they worked so hard to transform are diverting— or have already diverted—back to old pathways (see Chapters Two and Three for scientific explanation).

DAILY CHOOSING TO REFRAME AND REWIRE TO ACHIEVE YOUR VISION

In Chapter Two, you were asked to write a vision statement and were provided a vision mapping tool. Chapter Nine gave you many tools for planning, including "The 5 Step Performance Goal Setting Planner." Writing a vision statement does not necessarily produce a new business endeavor. For some people, succeeding at their current business or career is enough. However, having a vision statement and knowing what you must do to bring that vision into reality are completely different thought processes.

As you contemplate possibilities, you may feel excited, yet uncertain. For some people, discovering how to positively act upon their strengths and talents can be a challenging part of their journey.

Pursuing your greatness and your calling begins with understanding what motivates you and makes you feel complete. If accomplishing your written vision is crystal clear to you, congratulations! You are one of very few! Focus on and continue to reframe and rewire. Eventually you are sure to see your vision to fruition. However, for most people, knowing how to take their vision to a point of completion can seem hazy and uncertain.

In order to help you gain surety regarding the steps you must take to greatness, work on the next assignment.

TWELFTH ASSIGNMENT

Take time to write out 1–3 answers for each of the questions below to help you think about how to use your reframe and rewire to achieve greatness through routine and fulfill your vision:

1. If all obstacles were removed, i.e., money, position in life, obligations, etc., what would I really like to be or do?
2. In terms of a business or career, what do I love doing the most?
3. What positions, endeavors, or responsibilities have made me feel the most fulfilled in my career?
4. When have I found myself the most committed, passionate, and enthusiastic?
5. In what endeavors have I exemplified the greatest creativity?
6. Are there jobs or positions where I felt the most confident and decisive?
7. What have others told me I am really good at?
8. Have I earned any special acknowledgements for a job, endeavor, or project and felt like I could do it again?
9. Is there something I am good at that I often take a strong stand on?
10. What problems do I often see and feel confident that I'm equipped to resolve for others in the form of services, inventions, or concepts?
11. What do I like to do in my spare time? Could it evolve into a career or be monetized?
12. What skills or talents do I have that come naturally to me?
13. Recollect any school subjects or projects where I excelled.

14. What is the one dream or thing I'm good at that I might regret not acting upon in 5 or 10 years?

15. What traits do I have that could help me pinpoint the type of destiny I'm called to: competitive, outgoing, popular, entertaining, social, creative, charismatic, etc.?

16. What core values do I possess that could play key roles in determining my best direction?

17. What volunteer activities have I participated in or wish to participate in that indicate my passion and could help me determine my destiny?

18. What careers or endeavors do I see my friends involved in that appeal to me?

19. Concerning subjects of interest as they relate to career or business, which articles or books am I most interested in learning more about?

20. Finally, what would be most satisfying to accomplish in my life or career: helping others, politics, teaching children, motivating audiences, training leaders, bookkeeping, investing, starting a foundation, saving the earth, conducting research, etc.?

Once you have completed the above assignment, you should possess a fairly good picture of where to begin your journey.

However, once you begin working on plans to move forward, realize that your line of progression won't always be straight or predictable. While the original concept of your written vision may remain the same, the process and direction may change.

REFRAME AND REWIRE TIP #12
No matter what you determine to do on your journey to reframe and rewire, your path will always be mapped out in your daily routine.

In closing, remember that you will always reap what you sow, and you are the only one who can alter your destiny. No person, circumstance, or challenge can get in the way of your success unless you allow it.

I personally challenge you to put all inhibitions, excuses, and fears aside. Be one of the 10 percent and choose to be relentless! Then, *crush your bad habits for radical change.*

Below is a "Pledge" you can fill out and sign with an accountability partner, mentor, or coach to ensure that you will not put this book down and forget the reason you picked it up. Go to *reframeandrewire.com* and consider framing a copy:

REFRAME AND REWIRE PLEDGE

I, _____, pledge to design a consistent daily routine that will take me from level to level into a new destiny. I understand that big things do not create my future. Small things, diligently completed one day at a time, produce transformation. From this day forward, I commit to my new vision, routine, and goals in order to become the person I was created to be in every area of life. By signing this pledge, I officially set my course for Greatness.

Sign _____   Date _____

Mentor/Coach/Accountability Partner
Sign _____   Date _____

REFRAME AND REWIRE COLLECTIVE RESOURCES

REFRAME AND REWIRE TIPS

REFRAME AND REWIRE TIP #1

Consider how you can rearrange your current routine. New habits are never developed by trying to "fit them in" with your old routine. You will never have enough time. That is why we must create time for new things.

REFRAME AND REWIRE TIP #2

When writing your vision, think about four strengths you possess that will help propel you to your ultimate destination in your life or career. Under each strength, write out four of each: goals to work on and resources that will aid you in the process. Taking inventory will give you a clearer picture of how much you have going for you and reveal capabilities and resources you've forgotten about or laid aside.

REFRAME AND REWIRE TIP #3

Just as your body needs healthy meals each day to maintain optimum performance, your mind requires healthy nutrition. As you set up your new routine, don't regard the changes as changes. Instead, view your new "mind diet" as a necessary discipline to achieve your targeted result. Your mind, like your body, underperforms if you feed it a consistent diet of "junk food" such as TV, media, gossip, negative messages, etc.

REFRAME AND REWIRE TIP #4

When we observe positive changes as we gain awareness of our thinking habits, we create consistent progress. This progress produces a harvest that inspires us to sow positive seeds and to keep weeds out. The momentum we create by developing positive thinking habits pushes us forward faster than we might expect.

REFRAME AND REWIRE TIP #5

Managing "Heart Energy" and achieving Cognitive Consonance is not a "once and done" process, but a life-long commitment. Developing these qualities is a lifestyle. The only way to maintain positive heart energy is to become intentional about every moment of every day.

REFRAME AND REWIRE TIP #6

Taking revenge or holding a grudge is like pouring a glass of poison for the offender and drinking it yourself.

REFRAME AND REWIRE TIP #7

Focusing forward rather than looking back takes time, practice, and determination. The results can be compared to driving looking through the windshield of your car, instead of trying to steer a forward course while looking at the rear-view mirror.

REFRAME AND REWIRE TIP #8

Every thought, action, or role you choose either pushes you forward or holds you back. Create a routine that aligns your mind, heart, and emotions with your purpose and vision for a better future.

REFRAME AND REWIRE TIP #9

Managing Energy, Focus, and Time is more about managing YOU than it is about managing the obstacles you must overcome.

REFRAME AND REWIRE TIP #10

There are two kinds of people in the world: 1. Those who are interested in moving forward and have good intentions. 2. Those who are committed to positive change at any cost. Are you INTERESTED or COMMITTED?

REFRAME AND REWIRE TIP #11

Any project that takes effort and focus to complete will come together more efficiently when the right tools are used. The same is true with your new daily routine. When you consistently use the proper tools, your odds of succeeding are greatly enhanced.

REFRAME AND REWIRE TIP #12

No matter what you do on your quest to reframe and rewire, the path to your goal will be mapped out in your daily routine.

GREATNESS TIPS

GREATNESS TIP 1

To develop a new daily routine, you must be willing to significantly shift your current schedule.

GREATNESS TIP 2

Manage your schedule with goals of productivity, fulfillment, and stress reduction as you create task lists that promote feelings of purpose and progress.

GREATNESS TIP 3

Writing your personal Vision Statement empowers you with focus and clarity.

GREATNESS TIP 4

Focusing on activities that encourage you to feel grateful or accomplished reduces stress. As you design days built on constructive thinking, choose only activities and entertainment that push you forward toward your vision.

GREATNESS TIP 5

Ponder the mindsets you desire to change. Choose tools that will help daily equip you to keep your vision in motion.

GREATNESS TIP 6

Assignment #6 about forgiveness could be one of the hardest tasks you've ever completed. But the freedom you'll find when you finish this portion of the journey will thrust you forward as if a dam has broken and water that has long been held back is finally free to flow.

GREATNESS TIP 7

Realize that everyone has or will face adversity. You're not alone. The difference between being overcome by adversity and moving through adversity is to choose how you will process your challenges each day.

GREATNESS TIP 8

Having a written "Vision Statement" is not enough. We must committedly and consistently keep it in front of us and use in every area of life.

GLOSSARY OF TERMS

CHAPTER 1

Adrenaline (əˈdren(ə)lən) — a hormone secreted by the adrenal glands, especially in conditions of stress, which increases rates of blood circulation, breathing, and carbohydrate metabolism and preparing muscles for exertion. www.dictionary.com

Cortisol (ˈkôrtəˌsôl,-ˌsōl) — a glucocorticoid $C_{21}H_{30}O_5$ produced by the adrenal cortex upon stimulation by ACTH that mediates various metabolic processes (such as gluconeogenesis), has anti-inflammatory and immunosuppressive properties; levels in the blood may become elevated in response to physical or psychological stress. www.merriam-webster.com

CHAPTER 2

Neuroplasticity (nu̇r-ō-pla-ˈsti-sə-tē) — the capacity for continuous alteration of the neural pathways and synapses of the living brain and nervous system in response to experience or injury. www.merriam-webster.com

Synaptic Pruning — refers to the process by which extra neurons and synaptic connections are eliminated in order to increase the efficiency of neuronal transmissions. https://link.springer.com/referenceworkentry/10.1007%2F978-0- 387-79061-9_2856

CHAPTER 3

Cognitive Restructuring — Cognitive restructuring is a core part of Cognitive Behavioral Therapy (CBT). CBT is one of the most effective psychological treatments for common problems like depression, anxiety disorders, and binge eating. These are CBT techniques you can try at home to reduce problems with your mood, anxiety, and stress. http://psychologytoday.com

Cognitive Behavioral Therapy — Cognitive-behavioral therapy (CBT) is a form of psychotherapy that treats problems and boosts happiness by modifying dysfunctional emotions, behaviors, and thoughts. Unlike traditional Freudian psychoanalysis, which probes childhood wounds to get at the root causes of conflict, CBT focuses on solutions, encouraging patients to challenge distorted cognitions and change destructive patterns of behavior. http://psychologytoday.com

CHAPTER 7

Epigenetics — the study of changes in organisms caused by modification of gene expression, rather than alteration of the genetic code itself. http://dictionary.com

Quantum physics — (QM; also known as quantum physics, quantum theory, the wave mechanical model, or matrix mechanics), including quantum field theory, is a fundamental theory in physics that describes nature at the smallest scales of energy levels of atoms and subatomic particles. http://wikipedia.com

CHAPTER 11

Theta — A brain wave pattern that is between sleep and awake.

DOWNLOADS

CHAPTER 2

Vision Mapping Tool — *reframeandrewire.com*

CHAPTER 3

Cognitive Restructuring Worksheet — *reframeandrewire.com*

Affirmations Cards (The Power of "I AM") — *reframeandrewire.com*

CHAPTER 8

Energy Quiz — *reframeandrewire.com*

CHAPTER 9

Four Step Performance Goal-Setting (30 DAY PLANNER) — *reframeandrewire.com*

CHAPTER 11

Master List Template — *reframeandrewire.com*

Reframe and Rewire Template — *reframeandrewire.com*

CHAPTER 12

Pledge — *reframeandrewire.com*

ABOUT THE AUTHOR

MICHELLE L. STEFFES
SPEAKER, CORPORATE TRAINER, AND COACH

Using her experience as a leader, director, team builder, and business builder, Michelle has empowered individuals and teams with her coaching methods for more than 20 years.

Steffes has completed over 10,000 hours of study in neuroscience, physiology, and human behavior. She utilizes cognitive methods to accelerate growth, increase performance, and transform self-defeating mindsets.

Michelle is the Founder and CEO of IPV Consulting, Founder of IPV Group Coaching, Creator of the 5 in 5 Performance Coaching Program, and has been featured in a variety of media settings: magazine publications, radio programs, and national media networks. For more information, visit *ipvconsulting.com*.

ACKNOWLEDGMENTS AND DEDICATION

As I pen this page, thoughts of many people flash through my mind and my heart. The list would be far too long for me to include everyone who influenced my "Reframe and Rewire." Some people inspired me, and during painful times in my journey, others stirred a raging fire within me to become "more." I will begin by mentioning a few memorable names and end with many "unnamed" people who also deserve to be acknowledged.

My first dedication goes out to the Lord of my life, without whom I would never have made it through my many challenges.

Next, I want to dedicate this book to Mark, James, Carolyn, and Liz, who have stood by me, encouraged me, and supported me at every twist and turn in life. They are the pillars of my world!

To my mother, whom I love and cherish: Thank you for showing me how to grow through trials, stay true to myself, and laugh at life.

To my father (rest his soul): Thank you for teaching me to be bold and relentless in pursuing whatever I dreamed to become.

To my sisters Deb and Cheryl: Thank you for always believing in me.

To my mentor Carla: Thank you for always being there to support me in challenges and celebrate me in victories. You have been a solid rock in my life and have given me more than I could ever thank you for.

To all of my clients throughout the years: We walked together creating your journeys to greatness, and without you, I would be far less than I am today. You have enriched my life in many ways. I cherish each of you and so appreciate the opportunities you gave me to partner with you. Special thanks to those clients who were willing to share their stories in the case studies and testimonials in this book.

For my truest friends (you know who you are): Thank you for your devotion and constant support.

To my book coach Meochia and my editor Shelly: You have been a joy and a blessing to work with!

Finally, to all those who desire to be more but have been beaten down by life: I dedicate this book to each and every one of you.

- Those who have only known mediocrity but sense greatness in themselves.
- Those who have been "labeled" by others, which left scars on your hearts and doubts about who you really are.
- Those who know what they are capable of but don't know how to make it happen.
- Those the world has tossed aside, yet hope something greater is still out there for them.
- Those who feel "stuck" in life or career yet want to reach the next level but don't know where to begin.
- Those who have tried relentlessly to succeed, but continually end up exasperated and back at "square one."

Love, Michelle

ENDNOTES

1. Tom Ahern. "Search For Quality Called Key To Life." The Milwaukee Sentinel, 1981 October 24, Quote Page 5, Column 5, Milwaukee, Wisconsin. (Google News Archive)

2. "How Chronic Stress Creates Adrenal Fatigue." Women's Health Network. *https://www.womenshealthnetwork.com/adrenal-fatigue-and-stress/how-chronic-stress-creates-adrenal-fatigue.aspx*

3. R. Morgan Griffin. "10 Health Problems Related to Stress That You Can Fix." Webmd. *https://www.webmd.com/balance/stress-management/features/10-fixable-stress-related-health-problems#1*

4. "Neuroplasticity: Experience and Your Brain. "Brain World Magazine, September 30, 2017.

5. "Neuroplasticity: Experience and Your Brain."

6. Harold M. Schumeck, Jr. "Chemical Found in the Brain May be Key in Pain Control." The New York Times archives, 1979 December 21. *https://www.nytimes.com/1979/12/21/archives/chemical-found-in-the-brain-may-be-key-in-pain-control-derivation.html*

7. Anna Hedenus. "Pennies from heaven? Conceptions and earmarking of lottery prize money" British Journal of Sociology, Vol 65, Issue 2, June 2014, pp 225-244.

8. 2009, December 3. Seeing is Believing: The Power of Visualization by A.J. Adams. Psychology Today blog *https://www.psychologytoday.com/us/blog/flourish/200912/seeing-is-believing-the-power-visualization*

9.   2014 Oct 30. "Does your brain distinguish real from imaginary" by Dr. David R. Hamilton. Blog at Using Science to Inspire *https://drdavidhamilton.com/ does-your-brain-distinguish-real-from-imaginary/*

10. Citation Updated 2016, November 10. "A fascinating landmark study of placebo surgery for knee osteoarthritis" by Moseley JB, O'Malley K, Petersen, NJ, et. al. PainScience.com *https://www.painscience.com/biblio/ fascinating-landmark-study-of-placebo-surgery-for-knee-osteoarthritis.html*

11. Sanjay Singh, MSc, Patricia I. Johnson PhD, Robert E. Lee, et. al. "Tomography of cardiac ganglia in the adult human heart." ScienceDirect *https://www.sciencedirect.com/science/article/pii/S0022522396700946)*

12. Illustration courtesy Carolyn Steffes.

13. "The Energetic Heart Is Unfolding." HeartMathInstitute, July 22,2010. *https://www.heartmath.org/articles-of-the-heart/science-of-the-heart/the-energetic-heart-is-unfolding/*

14. Saul McLeod. "Cognitive Dissonance." Simply Psychology, February 5, 2018. *https://www.simplypsychology.org/cognitive-dissonance.html*

15. Leon F. Seltzer Ph.D. Don't Let Your Anger "Mature" into Bitterness. Psychology Today blog. January 14, 2015. *https://www.psychologytoday.com/ us/blog/evolution-the-self/201501/don-t-let-your-anger-mature-bitterness*

16. Dr. Eric Ibegbu, MD. *Our Daily Pill: Daily Motivation to Help You Discover and Release the Greatness Within.* Westbow Press, 1982, Part I, Day 9.

17. Caroline Leaf, *Switch On Your Brain*, Grand Rapids: Baker Books, 2017.

18. But They Did Not Give Up. *https://www.uky.edu/~eushe2/Pajares/ OnFailingG.html*

19. Source or Sources needed

20. Purple Motes: a journal of whimsy and hope *https://www.purplemotes.net/ 2013/09/01/parable-of-sower- arabic-life-buddha/*

21. *https://www.fastcompany.com/3036840/what-your-energy-level-means-for-your-productivity*

22. John Peever and Brian J. Murray. "What Happens in the Brain During Sleep?" Scientific American Online, September 1, 2015. *https://www.scientific american.com/article/what-happens-in-the-brain-during-sleep1/*

23. John Ericson. "75% of Americans May Suffer from Dehydration, According to Doctors." Medical Daily, July 3, 2013. *https://www.medicaldaily.com/75-americans-may-suffer-chronic-dehydration-according-doctors-247393*

24. Stanford University Press Release, December 21, 1979. *http://med.stanford.edu/content/dam/Timeline/legacy-1979_goldstein_A33.pdf*

25. Trevor Haynes. Dopamine, Smartphones, & You: A battle for your time. Harvard University blog, May 1, 2018. *http://sitn.hms.harvard.edu/flash/2018/dopamine-smartphones-battle-time/*

26. Trevor Haynes.

27. "Blue light has a dark side." Harvard Health Publishing Online, Harvard Health Letter, Updated July 7, 2020. *https://www.health.harvard.edu/staying-healthy/blue-light-has-a-dark-side*

28. Trevor Haynes.

29. "How Much Time Will the Average Person Spend on Social Media in Their Lifetime?" Adweek, March 22, 2017. *http://www.adweek.com/digital/mediakix-time-spent-social-media- infographic/*

30. Michael Schneider. "Only 10 Percent of People Are Natural Leaders. The Rest of Us Have to Work On Developing These 3 Qualities." Inc. September 22, 2020. *https://www.inc.com/michael-schneider/only-10-percent-of-people-are-natural-leaders-rest-of-us-have-to-work-on-developing-these-3-qualities.html*